SLOT MACHINES

THE HISTORY OF CABLE-HAULED STREET TRAMWAYS IN THE BRITISH ISLES

By

David Voice

Published by Adam Gordon

ALSO BY DAVID VOICE

How to Go Tram and Tramway Modelling, 3 editions
London's Tramways Their History and How to Model Them
What Colour Was That Tram?
Tramway Modelling in 'OO' Gauge
More Tramway Modelling in 'OO' Gauge
The Illustrated History of Kidderminster and Stourport Electric Tramway (with Melvyn
  Thompson)
The Millennium guide to Trams in the British Isles
The Definitive Guide to Trams in the British Isles
Toy and Model Trams of the World, Volumes 1 & 2 (with Gottfried Kuře)
Next Stop Seaton! 3 editions (with David Jay)
Hospital Tramways and Railways, 2 editions
Freight on Street Tramways in the British Isles
British Tramcar Manufacturers, British Westinghouse and Metropolitan-Vickers
Works Tramcars of the British Isles
The Age of the Horse Tram
Monorails of the World
Tram and Bus Tokens of the British Isles
Battery Trams of the British Isles
Mono-Rail, The History of the industrial monorails made by Road Machines Ltd, Metalair
  Ltd, and Rail Machines Ltd
Tramway Reflections
Shocking Solutions to a Current Problem
Seaton Tramway – It's Electric
Seaton Tramway – The Valentine's Day Storm
The History of Worcester's Tramways
Last Rides - Funeral Trams Around the World
All Dressed Up and Somewhere to Go, the History of Decorated Tramcars in the British
  Isles

A catalogue entry for this book is available from the British Library

ISBN 978-1-910654-11-8
Publication no. 115
Published in 2017 by Adam Gordon, Kintradwell Farmhouse, Brora, Sutherland KW9 6LU
Tel: 01408 622660

Printed by 4Edge Ltd, Hockley, Essex SS5 4AD

CONTENTS

HIGHGATE. A Cable Tramcar.

93.

Britain's first cable-operated street tramway. Tramcar number 9 waits at the upper terminus of the Highgate Hill Tramway in London

CABLE STREET TRAMWAYS IN THE BRITISH ISLES

INTRODUCTION

The first street tramway in the British Isles is generally accepted as that of the Birkenhead Street Railway Company, opened in the town by George Francis Train in 1860, although claims have been made for the Oystermouth Railway, opened in 1806 and passenger-carrying from 1807, and for the docks railway in Liverpool in 1859. However, the former did not run in the street, but alongside it on its own right of way and the latter was really a freight railway. In common with all traffic the motive power was the horse. As tramways spread over more towns it was apparent that the horses were the most expensive part of the operation and Companies sought a less costly means of power. In the search for savings there were some rather unusual choices that came to naught, these included clockwork, compressed air, petrol, diesel and coal gas.

The main contenders narrowed to electricity, steam and cable. Steam had a proven record on the railways, while electricity was in its infancy and went through many options such as batteries, current collection by conduit, stud and the winning solution, overhead wires. These alternatives have all been examined in books published by Adam Gordon. The one gap not explored in print has been cable-powered tramways and this book is my contribution to completing this aspect of early tramway history in the British Isles.

I have been researching the history of cable tramways in Britain for many years and when I started it seemed a straightforward investigation. However, as I delved deeper I realised that there were unexpected problems, the first and biggest being "what is a cable tramway?". A quick search on the internet comes up with "a conveyance that transports passengers or freight in carriers suspended from cables and supported by a series of towers". This is an American English interpretation and is a long way from my view. So for the purposes of this book my definition is:
> "A form of public railed transport that carries passengers in a carriage which is moved by cable haulage. The rail track runs wholly or partly in the street."
This definition excludes cliff railways, suspended cableways, people movers and monorails, all of which are sometimes called tramways.

It is difficult to pin-point the date of the first cable-hauled mode of transport. Like so many technological inventions the street cable tramway did not appear out of thin air. It was the application of previously used ideas with a new concept, burying the cable under the road so it did not interfere with the other road traffic. The idea of using inclines to raise heavy objects goes back over 4,500 years to the building of the pyramids in Egypt. Blocks of stone were raised using ropes hauled by teams of men. This system of moving items continued to be used and refined over the centuries. In 1777 the Tyrone Canal, Northern Ireland, built three incline planes to lift boats from lower canals to higher ones. They were not a success and were abandoned within ten years.

William and Edward Walton Chapman, brothers, were born in Whitby and grew up to become engineers. In 1812 they took out a patent for "a method or methods of facilitating the means, and reducing the expense, of carriage on railways and other roads patent". This rather cumbersome title was actually the earliest mention of a system whereby railway trucks could be attached to a moving chain to propel them. Though the wording of the patent is somewhat vague the attached drawings indicate a system where the trucks could be attached or detached from the chain. As far as is known the idea was never put in action, though later chain inclines used similar principles.

In 1824 William James took out a patent that added a little more detail. Much of the patent details using hollow rails to allow water, gas or other fluids to be moved. Later he mentions using the hollow rail "*as a trunk to receive rope, chains or rods passing from a standing engine or other machine, for the purpose of protecting them from external injury. In attaching them to such rail or tramways certain rods, rails, and endless chains, for the purpose of drawing carriages along the*

5

UNITED STATES PATENT OFFICE.

ELEAZER S. GARDNER, OF PHILADELPHIA, PENNSYLVANIA, ASSIGNOR TO HIMSELF AND JOHN H. GOULD, OF SAME PLACE.

IMPROVEMENT IN TRACKS FOR CITY RAILWAYS.

Specification forming part of Letters Patent No. **19,736**, dated March 23, 1858.

To all whom it may concern:

Be it known that I, ELEAZER S. GARDNER, of the city of Philadelphia and State of Pennsylvania, have invented certain new and useful Improvements in Tracks for City Passenger-Railroads; and I do hereby declare the following to be a full, clear, and exact description of the same, reference being had to the accompanying drawings, and to the letters of reference marked thereon.

My invention consists in forming between the rails of a railway-track an underground tunnel having in the inside a series of pulleys and near the level of the ground a longitudinal slot, (the whole being arranged in the manner set forth hereinafter,) in order that a traction-rope may be used for drawing the cars along the track without impeding the passage of ordinary vehicles across the same.

In order to enable others skilled in the art to make and use my invention, I will now proceed to describe its construction and operation.

On reference to the drawings, which form a part of this specification, Figure 1 is a sectional view of my improved city railroad-track; Fig. 2, a ground plan of the same.

A A are the rails, resting on and secured to the sleepers B B in the usual manner.

C is a tunnel formed beneath the ground and midway between the two rails A A, the top of the tunnel being composed of the two curved pieces of metal D and D', between which and near the level of the ground is a narrow longitudinal slot, e. The tunnel, with the curved pieces D and D' and their slot e, traverses the whole length of the track. Within the tunnel, and at convenient distances apart, are the shafts f, on which hang a series of pulleys for supporting a traction-rope, the shafts f revolving in suitable boxes on the opposite sides of the tunnel.

The traction-rope may be driven in any convenient manner at the end of the track, and may pass up the tunnel of the track in one street and down the tunnel of the track in another street, the rope being endless and moving continually in one direction.

A catch projecting from each car and passing through the longitudinal slot e is so arranged as to be under the control of the conductor, who is thus enabled to seize the rope and release it at pleasure when he desires to start or to stop the car.

The catch may be constructed in a variety of ways, and, as it forms no part of my present invention, needs no illustration or description.

It will be seen that the tunnel, with its pulleys and slot presents no obstacle to the passage of ordinary vehicles. The tunnel is made large enough to afford every facility for cleansing it of dirt, &c., which may fall through the slot e.

Disclaiming the exclusive use of a continuous tube with a slot on the top as a device employed in atmospheric railways, I claim and desire to secure by Letters Patent—

Forming between the rails of a city railroad-track an underground tunnel and hanging a series of pulleys within the same, said tunnel having a longitudinal slot near the level of the ground, and being otherwise so arranged that a rope may be used for drawing the cars along the track without impeding the passage of vehicles across the same.

In testimony whereof I have signed my name to this specification before two subscribing witnesses.

E. S. GARDNER.

Witnesses:
HENRY HOWSON,
CHARLES D. FREEMAN.

Above and Opposite: the 1858 United States Patent of Eleazer S. Gardner that sets out the main principles of the cable street tramways.

E. S. GARDNER.

Railroad Track.

No. 19,736.

Patented March 23, 1858.

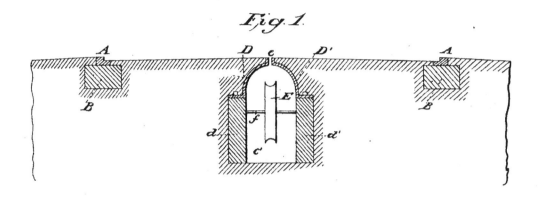

Fig. 1.

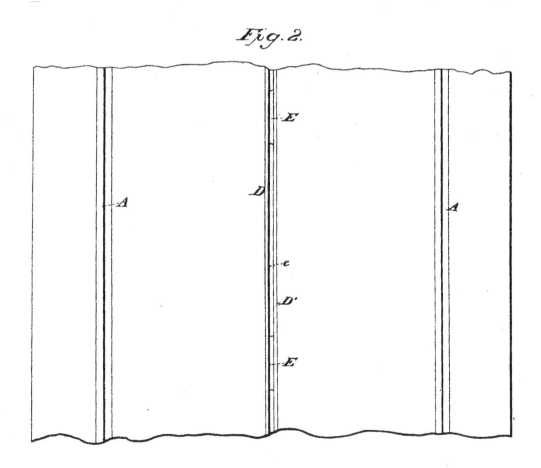

Fig. 2.

N. PETERS. Photo-Lithographer, Washington, D. C.

said railway by means of standing engines." This is the first indication of placing the rope in a conduit. The first cable railway using a continuously running cable (actually a rope) opened in 1826 as the Fawdon wagonway. Though it was used three years before, Maxwell Dick included the idea of an endless cable on a double track line to haul carriages in both directions in his patent of 1829.

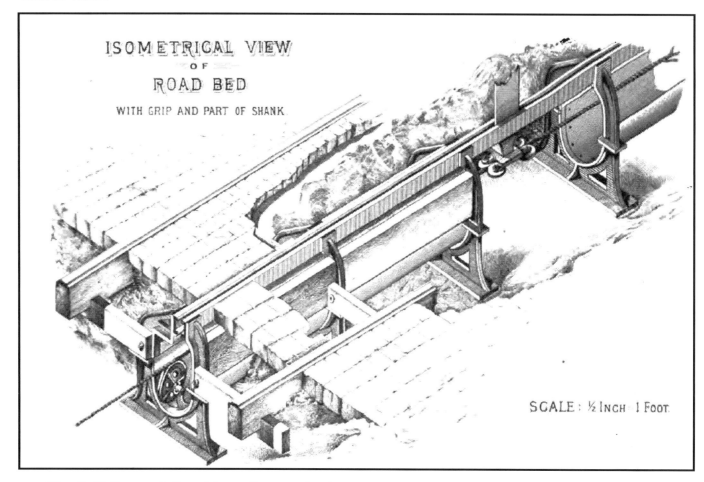

ISOMETRICAL VIEW
OF
ROAD BED
WITH GRIP AND PART OF SHANK

SCALE: ½ INCH 1 FOOT

The Hallidie conduit, cable, pulleys and grip as used on the Clay Street line, San Francisco.

The same system was used on the London and Birmingham Railway to draw carriages from Euston Station to Camdem Town where steam locomotives took over. Opened in 1837 the reason for the cable-hauled section was that an Act of Parliament prohibited the use of steam locomotives any closer to the centre of London. Cable-hauling ceased after seven years having been replaced by locomotives after a change in the law. A similar system was used on the London and Blackwall Railway (formerly called the Commercial Railway) when it opened in 1840. The rope that was used proved too unreliable and the line was rebuilt to allow use of steam locomotives. The next development came in 1845 when the patent of Robert William Brandling mentions placing a hauling rope below the surface of the track with a device to attach or detach from the rope.

A patent was taken out in 1858 in America by Eleazer S. Gardner who gave a more detailed description of "*Improvements in Tracks for City Railways*". The patent includes features such as a conduit with a longitudinal slot buried in the road between the tramway rails; an endless cable carried in the conduit; the cable running along one track and returning under a second track, being driven by a stationary engine; and a mechanism to grasp and release the cable controlled by a "conductor" on the tramcar. These are all the key elements of any cable street tramway. Once again this came to naught as no example, either as a model or full size, is known.

In 1870 two entrepreneurs, Benjamin H. Brooks and Abner Doubleday, had approached the San Francisco authorities and had obtained a franchise to build a cable-powered street railway in the city. It is not known if they, or Hallidie after them, had knowledge of the Gardner patent. Certainly the idea came as a new venture for the businessmen they approached for the required capital. This was such a novel concept that everyone they approached expressed an interest but felt that the idea was impractical. As a result, they failed to get the required money to build the line.

Andrew Smith Hallidie was the owner of a San Francisco factory making steel cable that was used on material-carrying overhead cableways, mining cable wagon ways and in the construction of suspension bridges. He purchased the rights to build a cable-hauled tramway in the city from Brooks and Doubleday. He set his mind to the problems of using cable haulage for public transport in the street. Being early in this field he patented many of his ideas, the first being lodged in 1871. His initial idea was to lay a line along the steep California Street and he contracted David R. Smith, an engineer, to carry out a detailed survey. After much consideration he completed his plans. He joined forces with William Eppelsheimer, a German engineer. Together they brought complementary skills and experience to the development of cable tramways. They chose to use "dummy" cars pulling the passenger tramcars, the dummy cars being more simple (and cheaper) to build. This enabled them to use readily available horse trams to carry the passengers. The original grip mechanism was designed jointly by Hallidie and Eppelsheimer (though only patented by Hallidie). It consisted of a large hand-wheel that operated a hollow screw that protruded below the dummy car, into the slot of the cable conduit. This larger wheel allowed the gripman (driver) to position the grip where it could grasp the cable. Then a smaller hand-wheel was wound which allowed the jaws of the grip to clamp around the cable and move the car. The cable ran at around 9½mph. It was soon found that the design of the grip had some inherent difficulties. Eppelsheimer developed and refined the grip mechanism, a complex mechanical device that allows the gripman to gently grasp the moving cable to accelerate the car and to release and later re-grasp the cable at complex junctions and passenger stops.

A view up most of the Clay Street line.

Hallidie's main role in the project was that of promotor and he needed to have financial backers before he could build the tramway. He invited three investors but kept everything confidential while the scheme was being developed. Their names were Joseph Britton, Director of Britton & Rey lithographers and mapmakers; Henry L. Davis, former sheriff of the City and County of San Francisco; and James Moffitt, Director of the wholesale paper house of Blake, Moffitt & Towne. However, in 1870 he unwisely told the editor of a local paper in confidence only to read about it in the next edition. This pushed him to move more quickly and, with the assistance of his associates, a Company was formed in 1872 and Clay Street was chosen over California Street, as the construction costs were less and it appeared a more suitable location. The new route was 2,800 feet long, rising some 307 feet. They established the Clay Street Hill Railway Company and stocks were offered to the public. The response was extremely disappointing, with just 120 shares being sold which were soon returned to the Company. The promotors made a working model of their system and this was lodged in their offices in the Clay Street Bank Building. It was derided by many who saw it, reinforcing the antagonistic response of other engineers. Most of the capital was raised by Hallidie and the three investors themselves. The franchise to operate on City streets stated the half mile long line had to be operational by 1st August 1873. Construction of the 3ft 6in gauge line started in May 1873. They began to run out of time and the first test run commenced at five o'clock on the morning of 1st August 1873, technically a day late, but a detail overlooked by the City fathers.

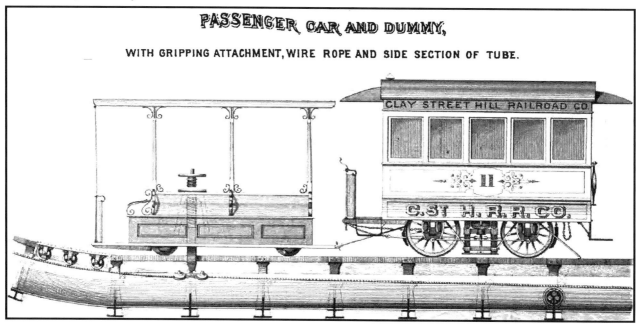

The Clay Street line cable dummy and passenger trailer.

At the winding house (at the corner of Leavenworth and Clay Streets) the boilers raised steam and the engines were started. The cable started moving and everything was ready for the test. At five o'clock in the morning the small dummy car was taken to the top of the steepest section of the line and placed on the rails, being held by the handbrake. The dummy was set at the top of the steepest section and was allowed to roll down the hill a short distance while safety ropes held it in check. It was then hauled back to the top. The grip was fitted to the dummy car. It is said that a locomotive driver had been engaged to drive the first journey, but when he saw the steep gradient he lost his nerve and handed the responsibility to Hallidie. It was manhandled back up the hill and Hallidie encouraged everyone to board the dummy. He engaged the grip using the hand-wheels and the dummy moved forward down the hill. There was surprise and relief when the journey down and up was made with no surprises. Further trips were made to operate the grip at various places, stops were made at the crossroads and the function of the turntable at the bottom of the route was tested. Everything had worked as planned. However, it was felt that the public needed reassurance and to promote the line all rides were free for the first two days.

The grip design proved unreliable. The cable would slip out of the jaws of the grip and the gripman would have difficulty relocating it and moving the tramcar. William Eppelsheimer continued to develop and refine the grip mechanism. His first change was to make the jaws operate using a bottom grip. This allowed the grip to be placed around the cable without grasping it, containing the cable but allowing it to run while the tramcar remained stationary. He also eliminated the two hand-wheels replacing them with a single lever acting in a quadrant. This was much easier and quicker for the gripman to operate. It was a success and the same basic principles are now used on all San Francisco cable cars. This showed that it was practical to run cable-hauled tramcars on the public highway.

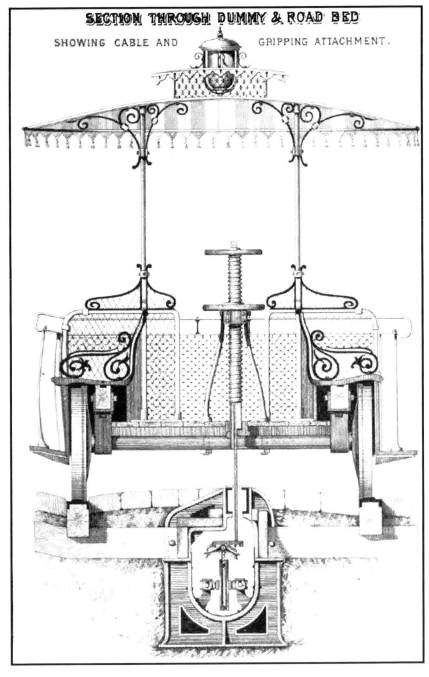

SECTION THROUGH DUMMY & ROAD BED

SHOWING CABLE AND   GRIPPING ATTACHMENT.

Cross-section of the dummy car and the conduit, showing the operating screw, grip cable and pulley.

Business interests watched the operation of the new line, particularly from a financial perspective. It was seen that the investment by the backers returned up to 35% dividend per annum. Not surprisingly this attracted investors who bought shares in new cable tramways. Companies were set up to exploit the inventions. In America the National Cable Railway Company and the Pacific Cable Railway Company were established to promote the patents the two Companies had acquired. Britain was seen as an ideal country in which to expand their business. To this end the Patent Cable Railway Company was set up. To advertise their businesses the National Cable Company and the Pacific Cable Railway Company both published a common booklet detailing the advantages of cable traction and listing all the 94 patents that were owned by the Companies. However, the two copies of the booklet were given separate titles. The National Cable Railway Company published "The System of Wire-Cable Railways for Cities and Towns As operated in San Francisco, Los Angeles, Chicago, St Louis, Kansas City, New York" while the Pacific Cable Railway Company used the title "Wire Cable Railways and Cable Cars". Both were published in 1887.

The booklets summarised the advantages of the cable system under eight headings:

1. The steepest grades are as easily worked as levels.
2. The cars may be stopped instantly at any point on the line, and started with promptness and ease.
3. The speed is uniform, and any rate may be established that is desired.
4. The method of working is noiseless and even, and unaccompanied by any annoyance whatever.
5. Perfect cleanliness of the track is secured, an important sanitary element in the system.
6. An unlimited capacity of increase at any time an increased carrying capacity may be required.
7. Perfect freedom from snow blockade, as the power is sufficient at all times to remove the snow as fast as it falls.
8. A simple and economical administration, unattended with unforeseen and unexpected emergencies.

Hindsight allows us to take a more measured view of these claims. Certainly the noiseless claim

Clay Hill Line with dummy and passenger trailer. Some sources identify the grip-man as Andrew Hallidie.

was, at the least, over-optimistic as there were often complaints about the sounds coming from the rotation of the guidance rollers. The absence of unexpected emergencies during the operation of the system carefully omits those expected emergencies, particularly stranded or broken cables, which would bring the whole of that section to a halt for many hours or even days. Like many ideas of the time it was a far from perfect solution to public travel.

There is some debate over the contribution of individuals to the development of cable tramways. Andrew Smith Hallidie's name is usually credited with building the first successful cable operated street tramway. However, it is not clear about the relative contribution of Hallidie and Eppelsheimer. The former tended to disappear into the background when the use of cable traction spread, while the latter was actively involved in other schemes in America and many other countries.

REFERENCES

Treatise upon Cable or Rope Traction by J. Bucknall Smith, 1887, reprinted 2010 Adam Gordon

The System of Wire-Cable Railways for Cities and Towns As operated in San Francisco, Los Angeles, Chicago, St Louis, Kansas City, New York, by The National Cable Railway Company, 1887

Wire Cable Railways and Cable Cars, by The Pacific Cable Railway Company, 1887

Street Railways their Construction, Operation and Maintenance, by C. B. Fairchild 1892, Street Railway Publishing Company, reprinted 2005 by Adam Gordon

The Cable Car in America, by George W. Hilford, 1970 revised 1981 Stanford University

CHAPTER 1

TYPES OF CABLE TRAMWAYS

There are two types of cable-powered street tramways. The continuous running cable, which is the more usual system, and the funicular system where the cars are permanently attached to a cable. The latter is more commonly found on cliff railways where it is not necessary to place the cable underground. In Britain there were seven continuous running cable tramways, all of which have ceased running, and two funicular type, of which one continues to operate.

CONTINUOUS RUNNING CABLE

These were found at:

- London: Highgate Hill Tramway 1884 – 1892 and 1897 – 1909
- Edinburgh: Edinburgh Northern Tramways/Edinburgh and District Tramways 1888 – 1923
- Birmingham: Birmingham Central Tramways Co/City of Birmingham Tramways Co 1888 – 1896/1896 - 1911
- London: Brixton Hill Tramway 1891 – 1904
- Matlock Cable Tramway: 1893 – 1927
- Douglas: Upper Douglas Cable Tramway 1896 – 1921

The key features of the continuous running cable street tramway are:

▶ The track and conduit

▶ The cable

▶ The winding house

▶ The grip

▶ The brakes

The whole system can only run by using all of these features. For clarity each will be examined separately:-

THE TRACK AND CONDUIT

By the time the first cable-powered street tramways were being built, grooved tram rail had become the world standard, replacing the original step rail that caused damage to other road vehicles. The first cable tramway along Clay Street in San Francisco used grooved rail, as did every subsequent cable tramway, and in this respect was very similar to other tramways of the day, usually horse systems. The additional feature of the cable tramway was the conduit that carried the cable underground. Clearly, running the cable in the open was not an option. It would have drastically interfered with the other road traffic. To attach the tramcar to the cable, the conduit had a longitudinal slot through which the grip fitted in order to reach the cable. So that the slot did not interfere with other road users, it had to be narrow. On the first line the slot was ¾ in wide.

The cable was endless and ran at a constant speed (usually between 7 and 12 mph) powered by the engines in the winding house. The cable was kept taut and, like any cable under tension, wanted to straighten out. Unfortunately, roads tend not to be straight and do not climb at a constant angle. To ensure that the cable followed the correct path between the rails it was guided by many pulleys. As the tramcar was pulled over the pulleys, the grip moved the cable away from the pulleys, so that they did not damage, or get damaged by the grip. When the tramcar had passed, the cable moved back to run in the groove of the pulleys.

Track laying in Edinburgh with the yokes supporting the slot rails and access holes for maintenance of the pulleys.

In Birmingham the procedure was slightly different. Note the tie bars between the slot rails and the running rails.

The initial expenditure on the cable system was considerably greater than horse tramways. Of the total initial capital cost approximately 66% represented the price of the track, conduit and pulleys. In addition to the grooved running rails a conduit had to be built between the rails to contain and guide the cable. First a trench, usually between two feet and three feet deep and around two feet wide, was dug along the centre line of the two running rails. The running rails and conduit were constructed using a framework of yokes. Made of cast iron, wrought iron or fabricated from steel, the yokes held the rails and conduit slot in position. The slot was particularly important. It was around ¾ in wide and relied entirely on the yokes to maintain its position, despite the pounding it got from the other traffic using the roads. If the slot got wider it became a trap for the wheels of carts and carriages (which were around ⅞ in to 1 in wide) with the danger of pulling them off their vehicles. If the slot should narrow it would stop the grip from passing, stopping the tramcar and probably damaging the tramcar and the cable. The yokes were set around every four feet or closer on complex track-work.

Delivering a new cable to a San Francisco cable tramway was a major event requiring as many as 54 horses to provide the necessary power to move the cable.

In order to keep the cable as free from dirt and grit as possible, the path of the cable was not directly under the slot, but ran to one side. Thus, falling dirt tended to drop to the bottom of the conduit. The conduit tunnel needed to be larger where pulleys are situated. For ordinary straight track, 12 in diameter pulleys were fitted every 40 ft or so to hold and guide the cable. For curves and changes in gradient, the pulleys were set closer and could be alongside each other. At the termini, the cable was turned through 180 degrees using an 8 ft diameter pulley. At the winding house, further 8 ft diameter pulleys took the cable at right angles to the winding drums powered by the engines.

In addition to the conduit there had to be an effective drainage system, otherwise in wet weather the conduit would fill with rain water. The drainage system also provided a natural cleaning arrangement with some of the accumulated dirt being washed down the drains.

Wooden former for producing the conduit tube when pouring concrete. The lever at the front allows the former to fold slightly on itself, freeing it from the cast concrete and allowing it to be slid to the next section to be poured.

Once the yokes and rails had been laid the conduit tunnel could be formed. Sometimes metal sheeting would be fitted between the yokes and the remainder of the trench filled with concrete or earth, the road surface being built using granite blocks or similar. On some systems the conduit would be lined (a special collapsible former was invented to assist this process) and concrete poured around the outside to give a strong foundation for the track. When set the former was collapsed and moved forward to the next section. The system included access holes with hatches that could be raised to enable maintenance engineers to reach down to check and repair parts. In Edinburgh a different form of access was used. A separate maintenance tunnel was built between the double track. It was 4 ft 6 in high and 2 ft wide and had access chambers to the pulleys and other equipment. This allowed access for repairs without disturbing the rest of the road traffic.

Delivering several thousand feet of heavy cable created difficulties. One solution was to use the cable drum as a wheel and move it by rolling it along.

THE CABLE

When Andrew Smith Hallidie was developing cable street tramways his experience in the manufacture and use of steel cables was essential. He was aware that the cable would need to be strong, resilient and capable of repair. The cable would have to be able to be repeatedly bent without unravelling or breaking. He foresaw that one of the greatest drawbacks to the successful working of the tramway would be damage to or breaking of the cable and to counteract this he developed a crucible steel cable with six strands of nineteen wires each (a total of 114 wires). The six strands were twisted around a hemp rope core and made a cable 3 in in circumference. Each wire was 0.062 in diameter, had a tensile strength of 160,000 pounds per square inch area, and was capable of bending over itself with a round turn, straightening out and repeating at the same spot without fracture. For the Clay Street line the cable was 11,000 ft long and weighed 16,000 lbs.

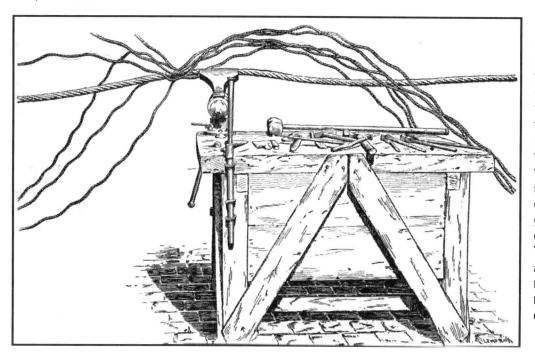

Splicing was a skilled and time-consuming task. First 30 ft of each end of the cable was unravelled and the hemp core removed. Then a strand was removed from the main cable and a strand from the other end inserted into the gap. This was repeated for each strand. The final splice was about 60 ft long while maintaining the original diameter of the cable.

It was generally considered that the maximum practical length of a cable was five miles. This would power two and a half miles of double track, though the Edinburgh system had a cable that was over six miles long. In operation the cables were continuous, however, in order to position the cable, it had to be dragged into the conduit tunnel. In order to insert the first cable some operators would firstly thread a light rope into the tunnel and fix it onto the winding drum in the winding house. The other end was fixed to the main cable. The engine would be started and the main cable would be pulled through the tunnel. The light rope would be wound around an empty cable drum for removal. Once all the new cable was in position the ends could be spliced together to form the endless cable.

The last stage in splicing and some completed splices showing how the extra strands use the space created by the removal of the hemp core in order to ensure that the diameter of the cable remains the same.

Some operators would drag the new cable though the tunnel using horses and a grip that fitted down the slot. The resistance to the cable was considerable and it is doubtful that this method would allow the whole cable to be fitted in one piece. Shorter sections would require to be positioned and then the pieces spliced together. Splicing was an essential skill, as damaged sections of cable had to be replaced in order to prolong the working life of the cable.

It was necessary to identify broken strands of cable as quickly as possible, not an easy task as the cable was hidden below the street surface. To aid the engineers the cable passed through a fork-like device at the winding house that was knocked upwards by a broken strand and rang a bell, warning of the break. This would be attended to quickly as, if the strand unwound too far, it could catch on a grip, dragging a tramcar out of control.

THE WINDING HOUSE

The unique feature of the cable tramway was that the motive power was stationary and did not travel with the tramcar, so there was no wasted energy carrying around a motor or fuel. The motive power could be as large as required. While this sounds ideal there are disadvantages. The friction caused by the movement of the cable over the pulleys was considerable and significant energy (on average 50% of the total energy used) had to be expended just to move the cable, without transporting the tramcars. Despite this, the operating costs of the cable tramway were substantially lower than the running costs of horse tramways. Even when the high initial capital costs were taken into account, the returns for cable systems were financially most attractive. "The Engineer" published some estimates in January 1883 stating that the profits for cable tramways would be between double and four times that of horse tramways.

The engines would drive the large winding drums that powered the cable. In addition to these drums there was also another large pulley that was mounted on a cradle running on rails. A weight was fixed to the cradle to pull the pulley to ensure that the cable was kept in tension and it allowed for changes in length due to temperature variation and stretch due to usage.

Inside the winding house with two steam engines (left and right) each able to be operated independently to drive the flywheel and main pulley that drives the cable pulleys. At the back is the tensioning pulley. The scale of the machinery is evident from the size of the engineer.

THE GRIP

The grip was a key feature of the system. Mounted on the tramcar, or on a dummy that can pull the tramcar, it was operated by the driver (or more properly gripman) and fulfilled three functions. It could be moved down to contact the cable and put it between the grip jaws, while allowing it to slide through them. It could be raised to move the cable clear of the pulleys so that, when the tramcar moved, the grip did not hit and damage them. When the gripman was ready, he tightened the grip jaws which made the cable pull the tramcar along the track. The jaws allowed the grip to slip while accelerating it up to the speed of the cable itself, 8 and 10 mph depending on the system. At stopping places, the gripman loosened the jaws and applied the handbrake to halt the tramcar, while the cable continued to move between the jaws. He tightened the jaws to begin moving again. The cable configuration meant that at some points on the route the gripman had to release the jaws from the cable and move the grip away from it. Usually this procedure was arranged to happen where the tramcar was on a downward piece of track, so it rolled across the area until the gripman could attach the tramcar to the cable again.

The first grip was designed by Andrew Smith Hallidie (possibly assisted by Eppelsheimer) for the Clay Street Hill line. It consisted of a vertical tube with a large screw thread on the outside and a smaller one internally. The gripman used a handwheel to lower the grip to the cable. The early grips had four small pulley wheels that guided the cable through the jaws. The gripman would then raise the grip, lifting the cable and jaws clear of the conduit pulleys. When ready to move, the gripman would tighten a second smaller handwheel to tighten the jaws. The friction of the moving cable on the jaws pulled the tramcar along until it travelled at the same speed as the cable.

On the first cable street tramway, the Clay Street Hill Railroad, Andrew Smith Hallidie used "dummy" cars with grips to haul passenger trailers.

On some systems the grip was fitted to a separate "dummy" to which the passenger trailer was attached. Some dummies had seating for passengers in addition to those seated in the trailer (some trailers were known to carry as many as forty-four passengers, most of whom had to stand).

In use, it was found that the Hallidie design, called a bottom grip, was prone to allowing the cable to slip out of the grip causing the tramcar to slow down and stop (uphill) or run away (downhill). As further cable tramways were built in America, other inventors came up with different designs. The favourite was a side grip where the running cable ran between jaws set above and below the cable. The most successful was that patented by William Eppelsheimer, a design still in use on the San Francisco cable car system. This is operated by a single large lever. Fully forward opens the jaws and releases the cable. Pulled vertical slightly tightens the jaws, holding the cable in the grip, but allowing it to slide through. Finally, fully back tightens the jaws so that the cable tows the tramcar along.

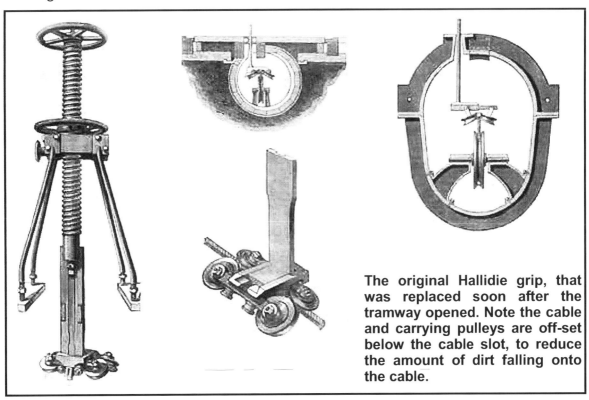

The original Hallidie grip, that was replaced soon after the tramway opened. Note the cable and carrying pulleys are off-set below the cable slot, to reduce the amount of dirt falling onto the cable.

THE BRAKES

When the tramcars were attached to the cable the maximum speed they could reach was the same as the speed of the cable, 8 to 10 mph. However, there were occasions when the tramcar was released from the cable and coasted along. Where the configuration of the cable required it, the gripman would release the cable and allow the tramcar to travel by gravity. He would use the foot brake on the tramcar to control the speed and then attach the car back to the cable. The footbrake was similar to that on a car, it operated on the wheels. In addition to the footbrake the tramcar also had an emergency brake operated by a lever. This either operated a clamp that gripped the slot or that drove a steel wedge into the slot bringing the tramcar to a sudden halt.

DISADVANTAGES

Although the cable tramway system was considerably more profitable than the horse tramways, there were still disadvantages. The first was the life of the cable. In use, the cable became worn or damaged and required regular replacing. It was routine for the cable to be inspected as the tramway operated. An engineer in the winding house would inspect the cable, as it passed over the winding drum, looking for damage. Any such part would be noted and when the tramway closed at night the cable would be run to bring the damaged section to the winding house where it would be cut out and a new section of cable spliced in place. The splice itself would be around 60 ft long. It had to be the same diameter as the new cable in order not to catch onto the grip. The central rope core would be removed and the splice used the space created. If the cable was worn beyond economic repair it was time to replace the full cable. A new cable would be taken into the winding house with an empty drum next to it. The old cable would be cut and a temporary splice made to the new cable. The engine would be started and the old cable dragged out pulling the new cable behind it. When the end of the new cable reappeared in the winding house the cable would be stopped the old one removed and the ends of the new cable spliced together.

An early view of the first street cable line, the Clay Street Hill Railroad, built in San Francisco by Andrew Hallidie. Note the offset slot for the grip, in order to minimise the fall of dirt onto the cable and the twin turntable arrangement for changing tracks and turning the cars. The passenger trailers were hauled by "dummy" grip cars, that also carried passengers.

Repairing or replacing the cable took time and, if it was urgent, would bring the system to a halt, but there was another more serious issue. If one strand of the cable broke it could catch on a grip, unravel and bind on the grip. This prevented the gripman from loosening the cable and he was unable to bring his tramcar to a halt. There were occasions when the runaway tramcar would collide with cars in front and push them to the terminus when they would all hit the end of the rails causing injury and damage. The same consequences would happen if the cable had a sudden slack and managed to wind itself around the grip. Thankfully both were rare events.

THE FUNICULAR SYSTEM

Most of the street-running cable powered tramways in the British Isles used the Hallidie system. However, two of them used the Funicular System. These were the Swansea Constitution Hill Tramway and the Great Orme Tramway. The latter is the only surviving operating street cable tramway in the United Kingdom. The major difference between the Hallidie system and the funicular was that the funicular had just two tramcars for each cable and they were permanently attached to each end. The cable was not continuously running, when it was time to move the tramcars, the cable started and both cars moved at the same time, one up and one down.

Like the Hallidie system the funicular street tramway relied on a winding house alongside the track that provided the power to drive the cable (some cliff funiculars use water balance to power the cars, but this was never used on street cable tramways in the British Isles). This meant that the tram attendant (neither a gripman nor a driver) would have to communicate with the winchman in the winding house to indicate when his tramcar was ready to move. On receiving the signal from both tramcars the winchman would start the engine. More details of the communication systems are given in the description of the Great Orme Tramway.

One of the key features distinguishing a funicular system from a continuous running cable tramway is a single or interlaced track with a central passing place. Here on the Great Orme Tramway the lower section tramcars pass at the halfway loop. This photograph was taken some years ago as can be seen from the overhead wires still being used for communication.

DICK, KERR AND COMPANY LIMITED

When the opportunity for developing cable tramways in Britain arose, the Patent Cable Tramway Corporation Limited (PCTCL) had already acquired the rights to the Hallidie and other cable tramway patents. The first tramway, that up Highgate Hill, in London was built by a subsidiary of PCTCL. As explained in chapter 4 the Company got into financial difficulties in 1887 and went bankrupt. Dick, Kerr and Company Limited purchased all the UK patents from the liquidator. The

Dick, Kerr Company manufactured tracks, grips, winding engines and other machinery and arranged for sub-contractors to supply other parts such as the cable, boilers and buildings, as well as the tramcars initially.

They were involved in almost all the street cable tramways built in this country. The exceptions were Birmingham (as it was built just before PCTCL went into liquidation), Swansea Constitution Hill and the Great Orme, the latter two being constructed on the funicular principle.

REFERENCES
Cable Railway Company's System of Traction Railways for Cities and Towns, 1881, reprinted 2010 Adam Gordon
Wire Rope Street Railroads in San Francisco and Chicago, USA, by W. Morris, 1883, reprinted 2010 Adam Gordon
Cable Tramways, by W. M. Colam, 1885, reprinted 2010 Adam Gordon
Cable Railway Propulsion, by W. W. Hanscom, Street Railway Gazette July 1886
Treatise upon Cable or Rope Traction, by J. Bucknall Smith, 1887, reprinted 2010 Adam Gordon
Street Railways their Construction, Operation and Maintenance, by C. B. Fairchild 1892, Street Railway Publishing Company
The Cable System of Tramway Traction, by The Mechanical Traction Syndicate Limited, 1896, reprinted 1994 Adam Gordon
The Hallidie Endless Wire ropeway Manufactured by the California Wire Works, 1898 Catalogue
The Hallidie Endless Wire ropeway Manufactured by the California Wire Works, 1902 Catalogue
The Cable Car in America, by George W. Hilford, 1970 revised 1981 Stanford University Press

A Clay Street Hill Railroad passenger car waiting at the lower terminus for its dummy towing car.

CHAPTER 2

CABLE TRAMWAYS – DEMONSTRATIONS AND RECOMMENDATIONS

INTRODUCTION

The 1800s saw immense development in commerce and engineering in Europe and America. One of the less desirable effects was the proliferation of inventions and accompanying patents proclaiming new discoveries, most of which were based on "little experience and indifferent engineering" (A Treatise Upon Cable or Rope Traction by J. Bucknall Smith,). There were also attempts to alter previously patented designs to avoid infringing a patent or having to pay royalties.

In early 1881 the Traction Railway Company became the National Cable Railway Company and acquired as many cable tramway patents as possible. In Britain, the first Company set up the Hallidie Patent Cable Tramways Corporation Limited that became the Patent Cable Tramways Corporation Limited, a subsidiary of the National Cable Railway Company.

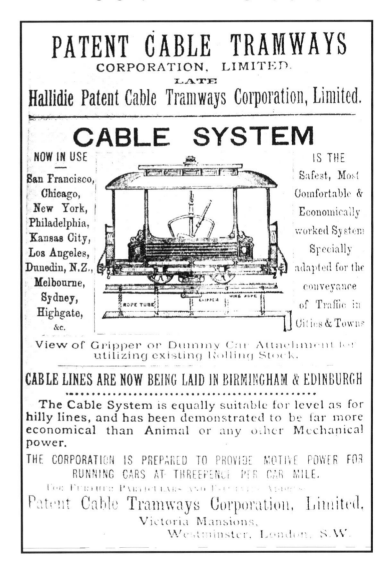

In 1875 Andrew Hallidie established the Traction Railway Company. The Company gathered together many patents, including all those of Hallidie, and it was not shy in taking legal action against anyone it felt had infringed the patents. This led to an acrimonious time until Charles Holmes, President of the Chicago City Railway, suggested that the parties should combine and make peace with each other and war on everyone else. They did so and in 1881 they changed the Traction Railway Company into the National Cable Railway Company to acquire and market as many cable tramway patents as possible. It also created the Patent Cable Tramways Corporation in Britain to do the same. J. Bucknall Smith considered that the consequence of these moves was to load a high cost on the development of cable tramways, both as initial payments and annual royalties.

In 1883 the National Cable Railway Company sought to expand their operation in Europe and chose Britain as a start, no doubt because of the common language and culture. Liverpool United Tramways and Birmingham Central Tramways both expressed an interest in cable powered tramways. Arrangements were made for demonstrations to take place on 25th September 1883 in Liverpool and later in the month for Birmingham. Unfortunately, there is a dearth of information about these events and no photographs and so it is not possible to determine exactly how the demonstration took place or who was invited to observe the use of cable traction.

The original Hallidie cable dummy and passenger car on the Clay Street line, from a contemporary drawing. The simplicity of the dummy is very evident.

LIVERPOOL UNITED TRAMWAYS

In anticipation of the demonstration, Liverpool United Tramways proposed to build a cable-operated tramway, using the Hallidie system, along William Brown Street, London Road, Prescot Street to Kensington. The demonstration took place at 3.30pm on 25th September 1883 in the roofed yard by the stables of the Kirkdale horse car depot. How the cable track was represented or what happened is not known. It seems unlikely that a cable conduit was dug, so possibly the running rails were raised to allow the cable to run under them and it is likely that a horse tramcar was adapted to be pulled by the cable. The builders of the Highgate Tramway, the Steep Grade Tramways and Works Company, applied to Liverpool Council to build the cable tramway, suggesting that they had attended the demonstration. However, the Council insisted on enough money being deposited to cover the costs of reinstatement should the tramway fail and other restrictions that the Company found unacceptable, so the cable tramway was never built in Liverpool.

No photographs or records survive of the cable tramway demonstrations carried out in Liverpool or Birmingham. However, this photograph of a cable tram built by Maschinenfabrik Esslingen for Lisbon appears to show such a demonstration, with the track raised on the yokes to allow room for the cable. The Liverpool and Birmingham presentations may have been similar.

There are no photographs of the demonstration of cable traction in Birmingham that took place outside Snow Hill Railway Station. This photograph shows a later cable tramcar in Colmore Row with the grounds of St Philip's Cathedral on the right and Snow Hill Station, the last building on the left of the road, just beyond the tram.

BIRMINGHAM CENTRAL TRAMWAYS

Around the same time the team went to Birmingham to undertake a similar presentation. The aim of the trial was "in order to form an idea as to whether the central slot rails would be likely to be a source of trouble in crowded streets". A report at the time said that "A short length of track was laid on Snow Hill, just above the station gates" and that it "has not given rise to any complaints." This infers that the experiment lasted at least a few days. It would seem that the Councils and the Birmingham Company were satisfied with the demonstration as they visited the Highgate Cable Tramway after it had opened in 1884. Birmingham and Handsworth Councils agreed to rebuild the horse tramway as a cable tramway, thus addressing the concerns of local people against steam tramways and the Council against overhead wires.

LEEDS CORPORATION TRAMWAYS

The licence for the Leeds Tramway Company to run its original steam and horse tramways in Leeds was due to expire in 1892. The Corporation was keen to gain control of the tramways and approached the Company in 1891 with a view to taking control a little earlier. The Company was not inclined to agree to that and prevaricated until the licence ran out, when the Corporation could compulsorily purchase the line at scrap price. The Corporation took over running the Leeds Tramway Company system in February 1894. This was a time of great change for tramways who sought a more economic source of power than horses. The Tramways Sub-Committee paid visits to other tramways in the country to see electric and cable systems in operation.

The Corporation decided they wanted advice as to the most appropriate form of propulsion. They asked the City Engineer to prepare a report on the subject. This was presented to the Corporation in March 1895. The report compared the pros and cons of cable and electric power without making any recommendations, this was left to the Tramways Sub-Committee. Inevitably, the members of the Committee were split. There was also pressure from two gentlemen supporting the Wilson Patent Cable system, where the cable was carried in a shallow conduit. It required less excavation when laying the line and so construction was significantly cheaper. They printed a 56-page report of their own "The Leeds Tramways, Cable (Wilson's System) versus Electric Traction with a criticism of the City Engineer's Report by John Sturgeon" of 1895. Of course it failed to mention that should the Corporation have chosen the cable system then the cable Company would have benefitted by £5,000 per annum from the Corporation in royalty payments. On the other hand, the Engineer of the Birmingham Central Tramways, a Company running horse, steam and cable tramways, criticised the design of the Wilson Patent Cable system suggesting it was flawed and that in Birmingham, the South Staffordshire electric tramway cost less to run than a cable tramway. It may be that the Birmingham Central Tramways management were unhappy at the financial information that Sturgeon incorporated in his report. He used the fact that the Birmingham tramway ran horse, steam, electric and cable systems. He highlighted the high cost of the electric tramway, though he was less open that the electric system was actually accumulator (one brief mention early on in his report) and not supplied by a power station. The reason for accumulators was that the Birmingham Council had objected to overhead wires, until they had taken over operation of the tramways, when they discovered how expensive the accumulator and cable systems were. They soon converted to an overhead power supply.

A sub-Committee was set up to consider the reports and representations. They completed a 77 page report that was submitted to the full Corporation on 15th October 1895. They concluded that the cable system would cost more to build and to run than the overhead electric system and the latter should be adopted. There was a lively discussion and the Leeds Corporation voted for the electric system.

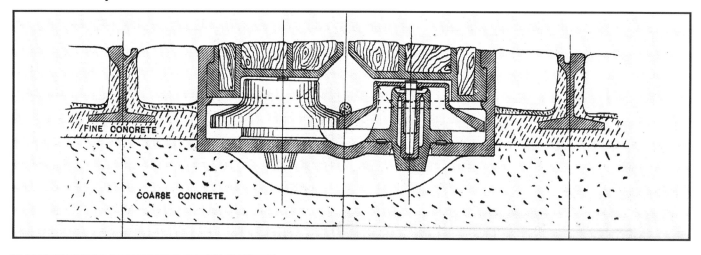

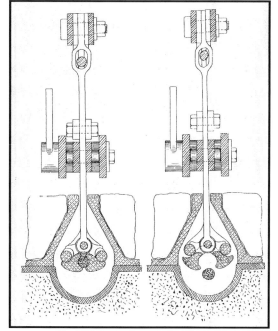

Above: The Wilson shallow conduit system that was being promoted by John Sturgeon in his unsolicited report comparing cable and electric traction for the Leeds Corporation tramways. The design relied on using pulleys mounted with a vertical axis to support and guide the cable.

Left: The grip designed to be used on the Wilson patent shallow conduit system. The shallow conduit system did not find favour in Britain and the design was never taken up by any tramway.

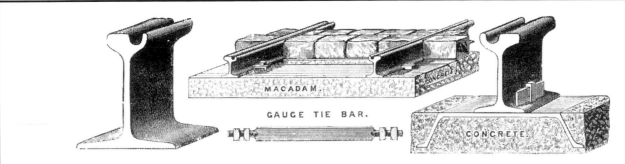

DICK, KERR & CO.,

ENGINEERS AND CONTRACTORS,

101, LEADENHALL STREET, LONDON, E.C.,

HORSE, STEAM & CABLE TRAMWAY CONTRACTORS,

MANUFACTURERS OF

STEEL GIRDER TRAMWAY RAILS,

Of all Sections from 35 lbs. to 100 lbs. per yard.

Tramway Engines, Winding Engines for Cable Tramways, Pulleys, Ropes, Cars, &c.

ESTIMATES GIVEN FOR LAYING AND EQUIPPING TRAMWAYS, OR LIGHT RAILWAYS OF ANY DESCRIPTION.

An advertisement of the time. Note the absence of any reference to electric tramways, as they were still at an early stage of development. Dick, Kerr had a great interest in cable tramways in Britain and it purchased the Patent Cable Corporation patents in 1887 when the Corporation went into liquidation.

REFERENCES

Leeds Tramways, Cable (Wilson's System) versus Electric Traction with a criticism of the City Engineer's Report, by John Sturgeon, 1895, Shallow Conduit Cable Tramway Syndicate

The Cable Car in America, by George W. Hilford, 1970 revised 1981 Stanford University Press

The Cable Car Book, by Charles Smallwood, Warren Edward Miller and Don DeNevi, 1980, Bonanza Books

Liverpool Tramways Volume 1, by J.B. Horne & T. B. Maund, 1975, Light Railway Transport League

Leeds Tramways Volume 1 1830—1902, by J. Soper, 1985, The Leeds Transport Historical Society

CHAPTER 3

LONDON

HIGHGATE HILL TRAMWAYS COMPANY 1884 - 1909

In 1881 the Steep Grade Tramways and Works Company Limited was established to build a cable tramway on Highgate Hill in London using the Hallidie system with a continuously moving cable and grips on the tramcars. The Company applied to the Board of Trade for a Provisional Order under the name "The Highgate Hill Tramways" to build the 3 ft 6 in gauge tramway, which was granted in 1882. The Company then set about raising funds to build the line. Clearly there was as much scepticism about the line as Andrew Hallidie had encountered when he promoted the Clay Street line in San Francisco. The Company failed to raise sufficient interest to continue, so they cut their losses by transferring the assets to the Patent Cable Tramways Company Limited in December 1882. The Manager was James Clifton Robinson, who had worked for George Francis Train on the Staffordshire Potteries Street Railway and then in America.

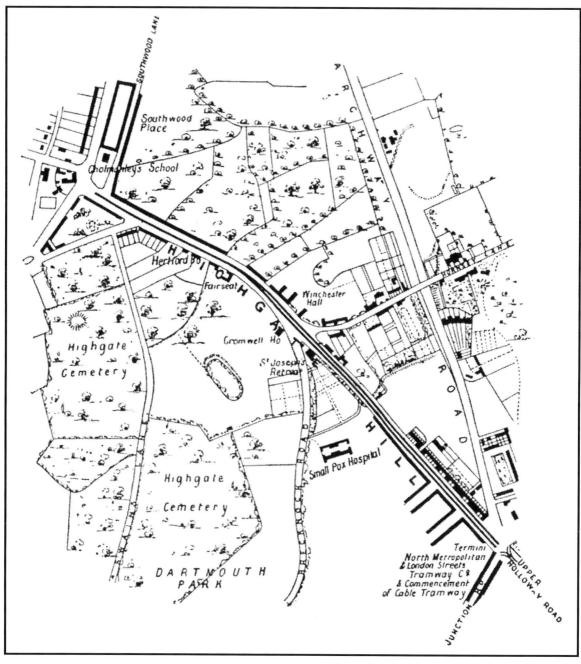

Plan of the Highgate Hill cable tramway, running from the Archway Tavern at the bottom right up the hill to North Road at the top left.

The opening of the tramway was celebrated with trailer number 2 decorated for the occasion and carrying distinguished guests.

The Highgate Hill Road is a steep incline and the tramway started down at the Archway Tavern and ended opposite the historic "Gate House" leading to Hampstead Heath, a favourite recreation resort for Londoners. The track was 3 ft 6in gauge and had a total length of 3,800 ft, of which 3,300 ft was double track and the rest single. The total ascent was 239 ft., and the steepest gradient was 1 in 11 and the curves varied from 250 ft to 3,000 ft in radius.

Highgate Hill is reputed to be the place where Dick Whittington, when he went to leave London around 1397, decided to turn back and stay. To commemorate this there is a statue of his cat (protected by some railings). Near the tramway route is the famous Highgate Hill Cemetery, burial place of many famous people including Karl Marx and Charles Dickens' family (but not Dickens himself).

At the start, establishing the tramway required some complex arrangements with limited Companies being set up. The English, Foreign and Colonial Patent Tramways Company was established to build and run cable tramways around the world. They had purchased the Hallidie patents and could licence other Companies to use them, including the Highgate Hill Tramways Company (established in 1883 with the aim of taking on the running of the tramway). At this time construction had not actually been started. Apparently, an American engineer, W. W. Hanscom, who had been contracted to furnish designs for the tramway, had missed his targets and was replaced by William Eppelsheimer (the Engineer who worked with Hallidie on the Clay Street line in San Francisco) and Mr J. Bucknall Smith (author of "A Treatise Upon Cable or Rope Traction, as applied to the working of street and other railways"). Land (about half way up the route) was rented where the engine, winding house and depot were built. Yokes were fitted every 3 ft 6 ins to support the rails and the 'Z' rails for the slot, which was ⅝ in wide.

The wire cable was manufactured by Bullivant and Company in Millwall and before splicing it was 8,000 ft long. It consisted of crucible steel wire, in strands, closed round a hemp core. It was 3 ins in circumference, or 15/16 in in diameter, and it weighed about 5 tons complete. The ends were joined to form a continuous loop and the splice was 60 ft long. The endless cable was carried on pulleys beneath the track, in a conduit of concrete 10½ in deep, 8½ in wide. The pulleys were fitted at 40 ft intervals except on curves where they were more closely set. The pits at the pulleys were 6 in deeper than the conduit and had drainage connected to the public sewer. It passed round two 8 ft pulleys at the termini, in brick pits. The conduit was relatively shallow to allow clearance for existing pipes laid in the road. The cable was driven by two independent horizontal steam engines made by Jessop in Leicester, each of 25 nominal horse-power, affording service in duplicate and the two boilers were by Babcock and Wilcox in Glasgow. The speed of the rope was from 5 miles to 6 miles per hour.

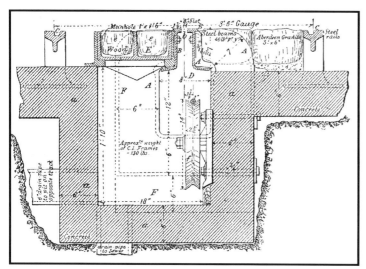

Cross-section of the track and conduit with support pulley.

It appears that the Company was uncertain as to which type of tramcar would be best as they ordered three types from the Falcon Engine and Car Works. They first ordered three single-deck dummy towing cars with three double-deck, open-top, four-wheel passenger cars. The dummy cars had some seating for passengers. The second order was for two double-deck, open-top, bogie cars that carried their own grip equipment and so did not need to be hauled by dummy cars. Soon after opening the tramway a further two of the self-contained cars were ordered. Construction of the line began in October 1883, and, as this was a new venture for Britain, it came under close scrutiny by the Board of Trade Railway Inspector, Major General Hutchinson.

Construction was completed in Spring 1884 and a trial trip set for 10th May 1884. The formal Board of Trade inspection was on 21st May and the line was approved for opening, subject to a list of restrictions including limiting the speed of the cable to 6mph. The Company invited the Mayor of London to open the tramway on 29th May 1884, when it became the first cable street tramway in Europe. Several of the tramcars was specially decorated for the occasion and the tramway gave free rides to the public for the rest of the day. The service enabled the trams to run at five-minute intervals.

An Engineer appears to have raised an inspection cover to carry out repair or maintenance work on the pulleys in the conduit. In the meantime a self-contained tramcar proceeds down the hill.

The winding house was alongside the tramcar shed at the depot. This meant that trams entering or leaving the depot could not use the cable, and horses were used to move the trams to and from the running lines. At its busiest the tramway carried 680,000 passengers per annum over 85,000 miles. Despite this it was never profitable. A major contribution to this situation was that the tramway had been staffed and equipped on the basis that it would be extended for a further 6½ miles to Finchley and Barnet, a development that never took place. Initially the fares were 2d. each way. Later, when the Company realised that the public were saving themselves 2d by walking down the hill, the fare for the journey down was reduced to 1d. Later, to increase business, both fares were made 1d.

One of the bogie tramcars with its own grip mechanisms. The lack of decency boards on the upper deck indicate that this is an early photograph. The fleet number was on the dash and not visible from this angle.

On 31st July 1884 dummy car number 6 with trailer number 3 ran away. The pair of trams had left the upper terminus and were passing the depot when the driver made an error. It was on the down line that the cable left the track to go around the cable drums in the winding house. As they passed the winding house the drivers had to detach their grips from the cable, coast over the section where the cable left the track and re-grip the cable where it re-joined the track. The cars would roll over the gap in the cable with the driver using a footbrake to control the speed of the car, where there was a 4 mph limit. In the case of number 6 the driver had failed to re-grip the cable, but thought that he had, so he released the foot-operated brake and the pair accelerated down the hill. At the top terminus the crew had failed to connect the trailer brake rods to the dummy when it was coupled. So when the driver attempted to apply the trailer brake there was no reaction. The brake on the dummy was not sufficient to slow the runaway pair and they ran down to the bottom of the hill where they collided with dummy number 5 and trailer number 1. There were passengers on the stationary dummy car who saw the runaway cars and jumped clear before the collision. The only injuries were to two passengers on trailer number 3.

Later that year, on 4th September, the grip on tramcar number 9 broke as it travelled uphill. Tramcars numbers 7 and 10 were driving behind car 9 and their drivers stopped their cars and went to assist. It appears the brakes of car 9 were not applied correctly and it ran down. As it was the uppermost of the three cars it collided with car 7 pushing it downwards into car 10. All three cars were slightly damaged, but no one was hurt.

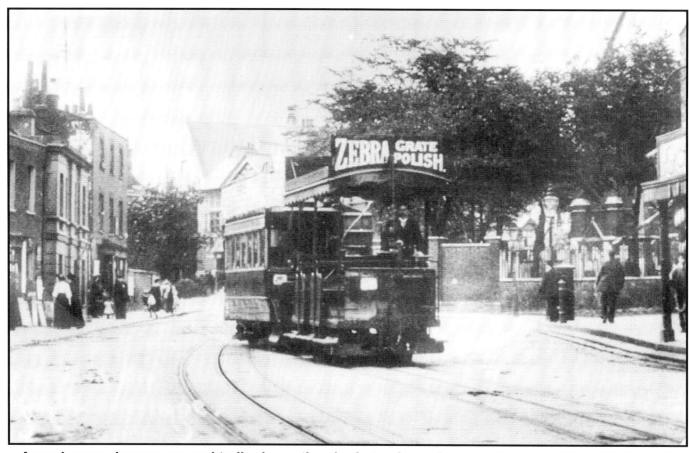

An unknown dummy car and trailer leave the single track section near the top of the hill. Conduit access hatches can be seen in the centre of the right hand track.

An early view of the tramway with dummy towing car number 5 and an unknown trailer. Note the absence of decency boards on the upper deck of the trailer, indicating the photograph was taken soon after the opening of the tramway. The conductor strikes a dapper pose, reminiscent of Charlie Chaplin.

There was a third accident on 8th January 1885 when tramcar number 8 ran away. The cause was deliberately going against the tramway regulations. These stated that the tramcars were banned from coasting down the hill except when going downhill past the winding house. In this instance a tramcar had left the upper terminus empty. When it was going down a double-track section, it was seen by the Manager who instructed the driver to release the grip and coast down until it reached the next single track section. Then he was to stop the car and use the upwards cable to take the car back to the top, thus saving a wasted journey. The driver released the grip and the car ran down the hill, but at the single track section it was going too fast for the driver to reattach the grip. It was early in the morning and the rails were covered in ice. The wheels skidded and the car ran uncontrolled to the bottom of the line. The two crew jumped clear of the car and it sped to the end of the track. Here it was slowed a little when the grips hit the end of the slot and were snapped off. It careered down the road and collided with a horse drawn local Council cart full of ashes. Surprisingly, no onc was hurt and neither was the horse.

Tramcar number 5 hauling an unidentified trailer.

By 1884 the Steep Grade Company and the Patent Cable Tramways Corporation were in financial difficulties. The Company had anticipated that the tramway would be extended to Finchley and Barnet (a further 6½ miles) and the fleet and staffing had been established with this in mind. The Companies were put in the hands of two new trustees. However, by 1886 the situation had not improved and the Steep Grade Company was wound up. This led to a turbulent period between 1889 and 1892 when the tramway passed through the hands of several Companies, with The Highgate Hill Tramways Company being prepared to take over in December 1892. The operating licence needed to be renewed at the end of the year and the Board of Trade told them that a further inspection would be required. On 5th December a tramcar ran away down the hill and collided with a stationary dummy car and trailer that were at the bottom terminus. The trailer was pushed off the track and it ran back along the Holloway Road for 200 yards. The Board of Trade ordered the line to be closed until an inspection took place. This put a stop to the proposed transfer, the licence was not renewed and the tramway closed for four years. Various attempts were made to gain permission to reopen the tramway but the efforts were thwarted as Hornsey, one of the three local authorities on the route, objected, saying they wanted the line closed. Finally, in 1896 The Highgate Hill Tramways Limited was formed that purchased the old Company. The Engineer and Manager of the new Company was W. N. Colam (who was later to become Chief

Engineer of the Edinburgh cable tramway). After the line had been repaired the Board of Trade carried out an inspection in March 1897 and again a few weeks later. It was allowed to reopen for public service on 19th April 1897. A steam pipe fractured later that day and this caused the tramway to close while repairs were carried out. It opened again the next morning and operated without incident.

On 23rd June 1906 a Metropolitan Electric Tramways type A tramcar number 115, working on London County Council track, ran away along Archway Road and crashed into several other road vehicles and another tramcar. Three people were killed and 20 were injured. Although this accident had nothing to do with the Highgate Hill cable tramway, other than happening to be close to the cable tramway terminus, the Board of Trade withdrew the Highgate Hill tramway's licence until they were satisfied that the tramway could assure them that the brakes of all the tramcars were sufficient to deal with all conditions. This was done and the licence was reissued. After this the licence had to be renewed every three years.

An early photograph of dummy number 6 and an unknown trailer. Later photographs show that the insubstantial rope was replaced by wrought iron gates to prevent passengers from alighting from cars until the conductor considered it safe.

Another contentious issue arose with the Board of Trade. The original Act of Parliament contained provisions allowing it to carry goods as well as passengers and, from the start the tramway hauled coal up the hill. Initially full coal carts would be attached to passenger trams and be towed up the hill. In 1890 a complaint was made about this practice and the Board of Trade stepped in and prohibited the practice. The tramway interpreted this to mean that they should not haul wagons using trams that were carrying passengers. So they continued hauling coal carts but with trams that did not have passengers. This raised another complaint and the Board of Trade clarified its decision by totally banning the towing of any other road vehicles.

The London County Council had started acquiring tramways within their area from 1894, although initially this was a protracted affair. Their objective was to gain control of all the tramways and convert them to electric operation. In the case of the Highgate Hill tramway, the line was purchased on 24th August 1909 for £13,000. By this time electric tramcars were powerful enough to be driven up hills like Highgate. Thus, conversion started immediately with the line being closed. The cable system was removed, the electric conduit installed and the gauge of the track altered to the standard LCC gauge of 4 ft 8½ in. It reopened on 25th March 1910. As a safety measure the conduit was strengthened to allow for special "slot" brakes which gripped the upper and lower surfaces of the slot rail.

THE TRAMWAY FLEET

HIGHGATE HILL TRAMWAYS COMPANY 1884 - 1909

Fleet number	Date built	Builder	Type	Number of seats
1 – 3	1884	Falcon Engine and Car Works	Open-top, 4 wheel	22/20
4 – 6	1884	Falcon Engine and Car Works	Single-deck, 4 wheel	16
7 – 10	1884	Falcon Engine and Car Works	Open-top, bogie †	22/20

Notes

† Cars 7 – 10 were equipped with grippers and so did not require the dummy cars to haul them. There is evidence of possible renumbering at some time.

Livery
Blue and white.

This Highgate Hill bogie tramcar carries number 3 and on a later page there is a photograph of another bogie tramcar carrying number 4. This indicates that the fleet was renumbered at some stage, but there is no record of when, why or what the new numbering was.

The Highgate Hill tramway was the first cable-operated street tramway in Britain and this meant the Board of Trade found it necessary to issue specific regulations to meet this new type of traction being used on the public highway.

Regulations.

I. The carriages to be used on the tramways shall comply with the following requirements, that is to say:

(a) Each wheel shall be fitted with a brake block which can be applied by a screw or treadle, or by other means, and each carriage, except the dummy carriages, shall be fitted with a slipper brake capable of being applied by the driver or conductor of the car.

(b) A governor (which cannot be tampered with by the driver) shall be attached to each stationary engine, and shall be so arranged that at any time when the engine exceeds the number of revolutions sufficient to move the cable at a speed of six miles an hour, it shall cause the steam to be shut off.

(c) Each carriage shall be numbered, and the number shall be shown in a conspicuous part thereof.

(d) Each carriage shall be fitted with a suitable wheel-guard to push aside obstructions, and each dummy and bogie carriage shall be fitted with a special bell to be sounded as a warning when necessary.

(e) Arrangements shall be made enabling the driver to command the fullest possible view of the road before him.

II. Every carriage used on the tramways shall be so constructed as to provide for the safety of passengers, and for their safe entrance to, exit from, and accommodation in such carriages, and for their protection from the machinery used for drawing or propelling such carriages.

III. The Board of Trade and their officers may, from time to time, and shall, on the application of the local authority of any of the districts through which the said tramways pass, inspect the stationary engines, cables, or carriages used on the tramways, and the machinery therein, and may, whenever they think fit, prohibit the use on, or in connection with the tramways of any of them which, in their opinion, are not safe for use.

IV. The speed at which such carriages shall be driven or propelled along the tramways shall not exceed the rate of six miles an hour.

V. The ordinary carriages shall be connected with the dummy carriages by double couplings.

VI. The dummy carriages shall be provided with gates which shall always be kept closed so as to prevent passengers leaving such carriages at the "off side."

VII. The carriages shall not be allowed to descend the tramways by gravity alone: but shall always be attached by the gripper to the cable, except when stopping or when passing the spot near the engine-house where the cables cross.

VIII. The conductor of an ordinary carriage shall not leave the rear platform of the carriage during the ascending journey.

Penalty.

Note.--The company, or any person, using such mechanical power on the tramways contrary to any of the above regulations, is, for every such offence, subject to a penalty not exceeding 10/-, and also in the case of a continuing offence, to a further penalty not exceeding 5/- for every day, after the first, during which such offence continues.

Bye-Laws.

I. The special bell shall be sounded by the driver of the carriage, from time to time, when it is necessary as a warning.

II. Whenever it is necessary to avoid impending danger the carriages shall be brought to a standstill.

III. The entrance to and exit from the carriages shall be by the hindermost or conductor's platform, except in the case of the dummy carriages.

IV. The carriage, or carriages, shall be brought to a standstill immediately before taking any facing point both on the upward and downward journeys.

V. The company shall place, and keep placed in a conspicuous position inside of each carriage in use on the tramways, a printed copy of these regulations and bye-laws.

Penalty.

Note.--Any person offending against or committing a breach of any of these bye-laws is liable to a penalty not exceeding 40/-.

The provisions of the Tramways Act, 1870, with respect to the recovery of penalties, is applicable to the penalties for the breach of these regulations or bye-laws.

Signed by order of the Board of Trade this 26th day of June, 1884.

Henry G. Calcraft,
An Assistant Secretary to the Board of Trade.

(Later) Regulations

IX. Every dummy carriage shall be fitted with a slipper brake.

X. No carriage shall leave the depot on any downward journey unless the cable is properly gripped and the slipper brake connections are in proper order.

XI. The conductor of an ordinary carriage shall not leave the carriage on the downward journey.

Penalty.

Note.--The company or any person using mechanical power on the tramways contrary to any of the above regulations, is, for every such offence, subject to a penalty not exceeding £10, and also in the case of a continuing offence, to a further penalty not exceeding £5 for every day after the first during which such offence continues.

Signed by order of the Board of Trade this 16th day of October, 1884.

Henry G. Calcraft
An Assistant Secretary to the Board of Trade.

REFERENCES

Highgate Hill Tramway, by T. de Courcy Meade - Proceedings of the Association of Municipal and Sanitary Engineers and Surveyors, Volume 11, 1884/5

A Treatise upon Cable or Rope Traction, by J. Bucknall Smith and George W. Hilton, 1887, Engineering.

Tramways – Their Construction and Working, by D. Kinnear Clark, Second Edition 1894

LCC Tramways Volume 2 North London, by E. R. Oakley, 1991, The London Tramways History Group

Hampstead & Highgate Tramways, by D. Jones, 1995, Middleton Press.

Bogie tramcar number 4 was originally numbered in the 7—10 series. The fleet of 10 dummies and tramcars was ordered to meet the anticipated extension of the tramway to Finchley and Barnet. The additional route mileage was never built and possibly, when the tramway ran into financial difficulties in the 1880s, the fleet was reduced by removing the dummy cars and passenger trailers. This would have saved on crew members, as both the dummy and trailer had to have conductors, while the bogie cars only required one conductor.

CHAPTER 4

EDINBURGH CABLE TRAMWAYS 1888—1923

EDINBURGH NORTHERN TRAMWAYS COMPANY 1884 - 1896

The Edinburgh Street Tramways Company was established in 1871 to build horse tramways in the City. Routes were built not only in the City but also in neighbouring Leith and Portobello. However, the horse trams were unable to operate over the hillier parts of the conurbation. Instead, the Company used small horse-drawn omnibuses. In 1884 (the year the Highgate Hill Cable Tramway opened) Dick, Kerr & Company Limited formed the Edinburgh Northern Tramways Company with the intention of operating cable-hauled tramways over the northern parts of the city not served by horse tramways. Mr William Newby Colam was appointed as Consulting Engineer and he developed new designs for resolving problems or improving on existing designs.

Dick, Kerr & Company had already applied for a Bill to build a 4 ft 8½ in gauge mechanical tramway, using any form of power, from Princes Street to Ferry Road, Golden Acre a distance of around 1½ miles. The highest part of the line was just after the start along Hanover Street and the lowest across the Canonmills Bridge. There were eighteen curves the tightest being 80 ft radius and the greatest 980 ft. One advantage to the City's Councillors was that the use of cable traction meant there were no unsightly overhead wires in their streets. Construction work started in 1885 and was undertaken by The Patent Cable Tramways Corporation. Owing to delays the line was not ready to be opened until 28th January 1888. By this time the Patent Cable Corporation had gone into liquidation and Dick, Kerr had purchased the patents. In their publication "The System of Wire-Cable Railways for Cities and Towns" published by the National Cable Railway Company, they listed 94 different patents they owned, taken out by 37 inventors. There was no formal ceremony for the opening of the Edinburgh cable tramway.

Reputed to be the first cable tramcar in Edinburgh, this shows one of the 1—8 series cars with the route board for the first cable route opened in the city.

There was close cooperation between the new Edinburgh system and the established cable tramway at Highgate Hill. Mr Colam, the Edinburgh tramway engineer, was also the Highgate Hill Manager and a number of improvements developed on the London line had been used in Edinburgh. The winding house and car shed were located down Henderson Row, halfway along the route. Apart from a cable break after a week's working, which was quickly repaired, the line worked very well. Eight double-deck bogie tramcars, numbered 1 – 8, were ordered from the

Metropolitan Railway Carriage and Wagon Company Ltd. In the winding house were two horizontal steam engines built by Dick, Kerr with boilers from Babcox and Wilcox of Renfrew. Encouraged by the success, the Company immediately commenced work on the next route. This was the Stockwell route that ran from Princes Street to Comely Bank. It opened on 17th February 1890.

THE ENGINEER 9th AUGUST 1889 Page 118

On August 5th General Hutchinson, of the Board of Trade, inspected another cable tramway in Edinburgh. The new line introduces many new features of interest to tramway engineers. The motive power for the new line is to be provided by the machinery now successfully working another line nearly half a mile away. It is anticipated that the two lines worked from the one depot, and under the same management, will yield a good return on the capital expended, as the one line working alone is working at under 60 per cent. of the receipts. The engineer of the line is Mr. W. N. Colam Assoc. M. Inst. C.E. and the contractors are Messrs. Dick, Kerr and Co London.

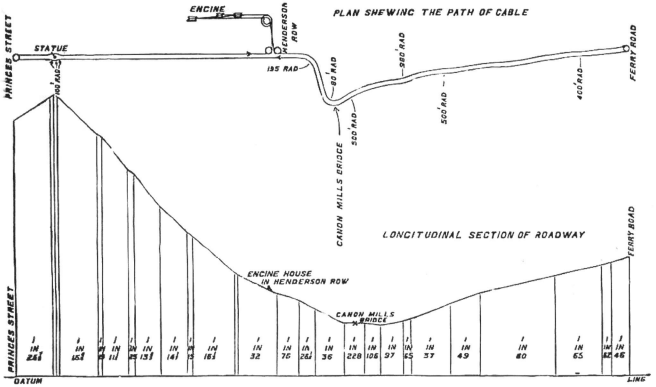

PLAN AND GRADIENT DIAGRAM—EDINBURGH CABLE TRAMWAY.

The Duke of Wellington's statue made by Sir John Steell with the Walter Scott Memorial in the background. This led to the saying "the Iron Duke in bronze by Steell". Cable trams are busy travelling along Princes Street.

Each line had its own endless cable and both were driven by steam engines in the winding house in Henderson Row. Tramcars for both routes were also housed in a common depot built next to the winding house. The grip slot on the lines leading along Henderson Road to the depot stopped short and drivers had to halt their tramcars and raise the grip through a small hatchway in the road. The tram would then be shunted in and out of the shed using horse power. Access to the roads in the shed was via a traverser.

At the point where the two cables left the main route a safety device was fitted to prevent a tramcar that was still attached to the cable from pulling it off the pulleys and breaking it. First, as the tramcar approached the gap, if the driver had not detached the grip it hit a lever that rang a warning bell. The driver was supposed to detach the grip immediately. If he failed to do so, the grip hit another lever that operated a metal bar (called a pawl) that moved across the slot. If the tramcar still had the grip attached, it would hit the bar which brought the tramcar to a sudden stop.

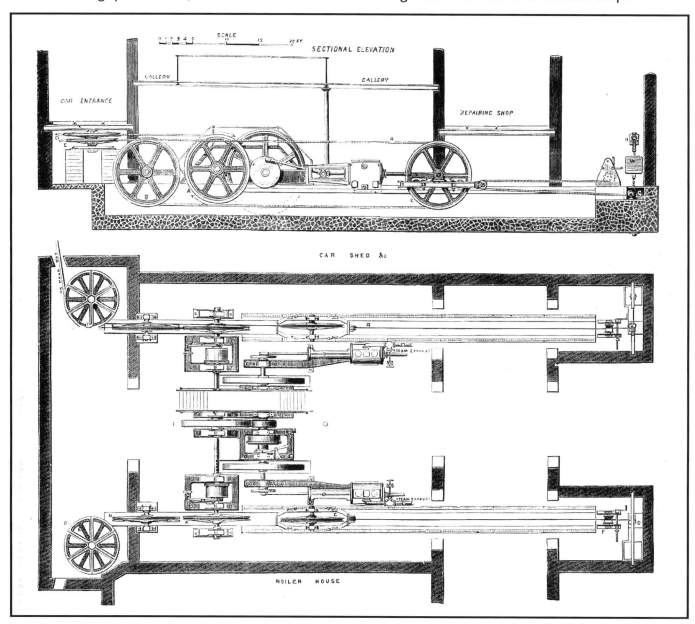

The driving engines in the Henderson Row winding house with the tensioning pulleys. One set of winding pulleys drives the Princes Street to Golden Acre route and the other the Princes Street to Comely Bank route.

Between 1890 and 1892 eight more tramcars were purchased to run the service at the required frequency. These were numbered 9 – 16 and were double-deck open-top bogie cars built by the Falcon Engine and Car Works of Loughborough. The final increase to the fleet was in 1894 and 1895 when two single-deck bogie cars were purchased. Little is known about these, although it is thought they originated in America. For unknown reasons they were not used very much, though they lasted until the Northern Company was taken over by the District Company.

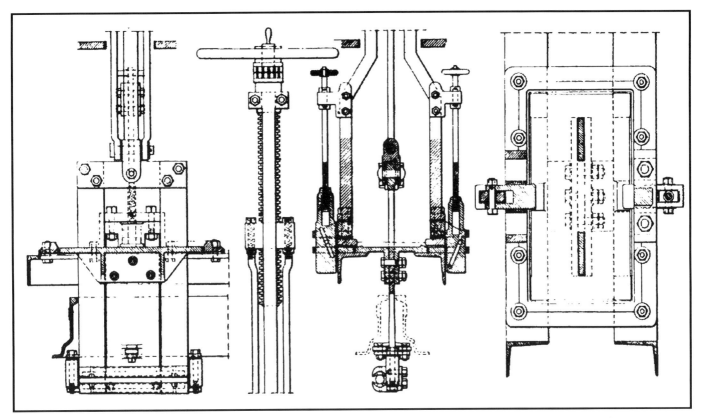

Above: The grip used by the Edinburgh Northern Tramways was designed by William Newby Colam and was the side grip type.

Below: Longitudinal- and cross-section of the track at Edinburgh showing the drainage pipes and a pulley pit.

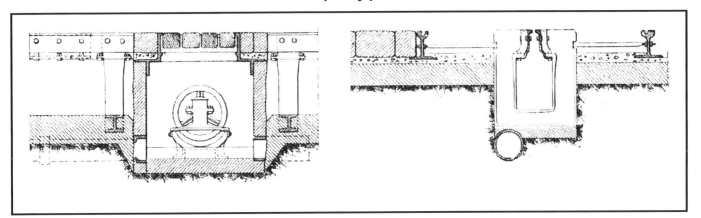

EDINBURGH AND DISTRICT TRAMWAYS COMPANY LIMITED 1893 – 1919

Dick, Kerr & Company established the Edinburgh and District Tramways Company in 1893 to operate the horse tramways of the Edinburgh Street Tramways, initially (from 9th December 1893) those routes within the city boundary. At this time there were complex regulations concerning the ownership and operation of street tramways. Local Councils were allowed to own and build tramways, but were not authorised to operate them, so such lines would be leased to private Companies. Alternatively, a private Company could build and own the tramway and then operate it. In this case the local Council had the right to purchase the tramway after a set number of years. Therefore, it took a few years for the Council to purchase the tramways from the private Companies. The line to Meadowbank was purchased on 31st January 1896 and two years later, in 1898, they bought the line to Portobello.

On 30th June 1898 the Council entered into a 21-year lease with the Edinburgh and District Tramways Company, a Dick, Kerr & Company subsidiary, for them to operate the tramway. The intention was to convert the horse tramways to cable operation. To this end two new winding houses were built, one at Shrubhill and the other at Tollcross. The Shrubhill winding house had

A tramcar from the second batch purchased, given the numbers 9—16.

three boilers and two horizontal steam engines. To lay the cable, a light cable was positioned by dropping it through the slot in the conduit and locating it correctly over the pulleys. One end was wound around the driving drum and the main cable spliced to the other end. The engine was started and the light cable was wound in, drawing the main cable into position along the conduit. When it reached the winding house the ends of the main cable were brought together and spliced.

In 1897 six tramcars built by George F. Milnes and Company, numbered 139 – 144, were delivered to the new depot, while a further 100 were waiting at the factory for sufficient space to be found for them to be delivered. The first section of converted horse tramway opened on 1st June 1899 from Pilrig to St Andrews Street. The tramcars were then run for three hours giving free rides to the public. However, the line then closed for some days while essential work was undertaken. The horse tram service continued on the route using a temporary track alongside the cable tramway. Successful trials of the whole route to Braids Hill were undertaken on 1st October and on a few following days. The Board of Trade inspection took place on 12th October. It was undertaken by Sir Francis Marindin, Chief Inspector, who was accompanied by Sir Andrew McDonald, Lord Provost of Edinburgh, and several members of the Corporation; Mr. Hall Blyth, C.E.; Mr. Pitcairn, General Manager for the Edinburgh and District Tramway Company, Mr. John Kerr, representing Messrs. Dick, Kerr, and Company; Mr. Colam and Mr. Cooper, the City's Engineers; and Mr. Arthur L. Shackleford, of Brown, Marshall and Company Limited, Birmingham, the makers of the cars. The inspection was a success and the line passed for operation which then opened to the public on 26th October 1899.

The route was worked by three main cables, approximately 4½, 3½, and 2¾ miles long, each of which was 3¾ in. in circumference and made up of ninety steel wires, each capable of withstanding a strain of 75 tons per square inch. The principal power station at Tollcross powered two of the cables, while the third was powered from the Shrubhill winding house. The Tollcross winding house had three sets of 500 horse-power engines, although when opened only one was required.

Above: Tramcar number 143 appears to have been recently delivered, with a smart driver and conductor proudly standing next to it.

Below: Number 182 was one of the batch built by Brown, Marshall and Company and delivered between 1899 and 1901. There appear to be three conductors for this car, perhaps they are expecting a rush!

One of the other engines was needed for future planned routes and the third was there as a reserve. Tramcars were moved in and out of the depots by auxiliary cables.

The routes to the south-east from Leith Street to Nether Liberton and east-west from Salisbury to Church Hill, then north to Tollcross all opened on 23rd May 1900, having been inspected by Col. Yorke the previous day. On the 9th August Col. Yorke inspected the extension from Princes Street to Haymarket and the public service started the next day. This was followed on 10th September when the extension to Murrayfield was opened to public service, however it was not inspected until Col. Von Donop visited the City on 14th December. He also inspected the line to Gorgie and the Morrison Street link that had not been inaugurated pending the Inspector's visit. They were opened to the public the following day. In September 1900 the practice of hailing tramcars anywhere along their routes ceased and the cars would only halt at designated stops, which were marked by signs attached to lamp-posts.

The final sections of tramway were then converted which meant that by 1901 the majority of the cable system had been built and was in public service. The whole system was finally completed by 1918 with over 25 miles of cable tramway routes and over 200 tramcars. The complex geography of the city meant that the system required a large number of auxiliary cables to assist tramcars over junctions and tight curves. There were 13 main cables and 12 auxiliary cables, all driven from the four winding houses.

In 1902 the tramway Company had an argument with the Council regarding running a Sunday service. The Council was strictly against it, while the Company wanted the income it generated. The reason for the financial need was in part due to the Council. The lease for the tramway incorporated a payment of 7% per annum of the construction costs. Whilst the Company had ac-

The interior of the Tollcross winding house showing the steam engines, the main drive with its many drive belts and, on the far left, the pulley wheels that drove the traction cable.

Next to Tollcross winding house was a tramcar depot with 18 tracks, all connected by the traverser. The depot sloped slightly to assist the manhandling of cars out

cepted the condition, they found that their profit was absorbed by this cost. They particularly argued over the sum that the Council had determined as being their cost of building the tramway. The Council set the sum at 30% higher than the Company felt was correct. Some changes were made, though it was not until 1908 that deferred shareholders got a dividend from the tramway.

When the new Company took over the running of the tramway it put its name on the trams as shown in this photograph.

There was a significant move in 1905. The tramway had been restricted to running at 8 mph (6 mph on some routes) by the Act authorising the tramway. Normally the Act authorising a tramway had provisions to enable the Board of Trade to determine the speed of the tramcars. However, the Act enabling the Edinburgh tramway had fixed the maximum speed allowed. It was necessary for a Provisional Order to be passed that modified the original Act. It went through unopposed and the maximum speed of the tramway was to be set by the Board of Trade. They agreed to 12 mph on most routes, but where there were safety issues the limit was put at 10 mph or 8 mph.

An animated scene in Princes Street demonstrating the frequency of the tram service and the lack of other traffic in the street.

As part of the agreement with the Council, the Company acquired the 18 tramcars owned by the Edinburgh Northern Tramways Company. However, it was felt that these trams were too small for the ambitions of the Edinburgh and District Company. The Shrubhill workshops were given the project to design and build a larger tramcar for use on the new cable lines. The result was car number 112. Six cars were ordered from G. F. Milnes & Company Limited and were broadly to the new design, but were 17 in shorter. They were delivered in 1897 and numbered 139 – 144, while the cars acquired from the Edinburgh Northern Tramway were re-numbered 121 – 138. Between 1899 and 1900, 33 more tramcars were purchased from G. F. Milnes & Company Limited and a further 118 between 1899 and 1901 from Brown, Marshall and Company. Another 20 cars were ordered in 1903 (numbers 209 to 228) this time from the Electric Railway & Carriage Works Limited. In 1906 the Shrubhill workshops began making tramcars. There were five cars made by converting horse trams to open-top bogie cars and sixteen new cars. Altogether there were 217 cable tramcars built for the tramway operating over fourteen different routes, though not all trams lasted to the end of operation.

The tramcars were fitted with two grips, one at each end. The driver could operate either one whichever end he was occupying. Indeed, some operations requiring moving between main cables and auxiliary cables meant changing grip in order to complete the move. The movement across junctions could be complex and sometimes cars were stranded, when horses would come to the aid and move the tramcar into a position where the appropriate cable could be gripped. This meant that for part of the journey the tramcar would be propelled by the rear grip. There was another advantage - if one of the grips became disabled the tram could still be moved using the second grip. To assist the drivers, the setts in the road incorporated special patterns that gave instructions to the driver. There were ten different designs, each with its own specific meaning. For example; one meant change cables and leave using the newly picked-up cable. Another meant drop the cable and leave by gravity ready to pick up the next cable. These assisted the driver to carry out the correct manoeuvre in the correct place.

In addition, the system had a series of "pawls" at places where the main cable had to be disengaged. The pawl was a device to block the passage of the grip. If a tramcar hit the pawl it would come to an abrupt halt, shaking the passengers, but this would prevent the car from moving over the position where the main cable left the track. The consequence would be to pull the cable from the pulleys and possibly out of the conduit, with consequent delays while repairs took place. Due to the complexity of the track-work there were a significant number of pawls, which were actioned more frequently than desired, causing damage to tramcars and their grips. It was found that by allowing more cable changes using gravity to pass over the change area the number of incidents was significantly reduced.

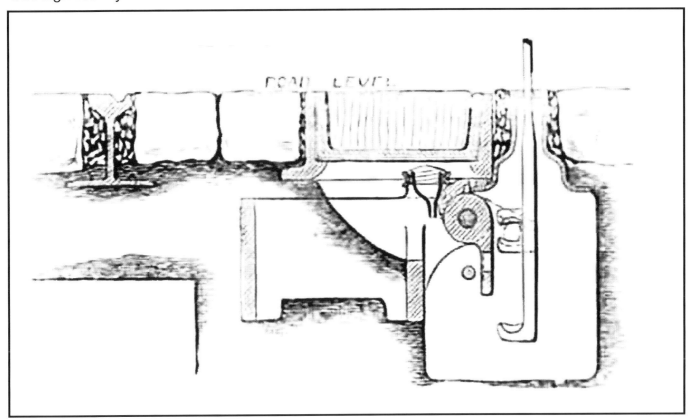

The emergency stop pawl. If the grip continued to hold the cable when it reached the pawl, the cable would lift the pawl creating an obstruction (shown by the dotted lines) and stopping the grip from any further movement.

The Council obtained an Act to build a tramway from Leith Street to Canonmills in 1906. By this time the Council was concerned by the high capital cost of laying cable tramways and started looking at electric power. One major concern, spoiling the streets with overhead wires, was still an issue. The stud contact system was investigated. This method of power supply used metal studs in the road with a long skate under the tramcars. As the tramcar passed over a stud, the skate would switch it on (usually by magnetism) and pass power to the tram. When the tram had passed over the stud, it would switch off. A Committee looked into the various systems available and they were in favour of the Griffiths-Bedell (G-B) system. However, part of the new route was to use existing cable tram track. It was impossible to lay a stud system over the existing cable conduit. If electricity was to be used the only option was overhead wire, which the Council was against, therefore the Council decided to lay all of it as a cable tramway. The final horse tram route, Tollcross to Craiglockhart was converted to cable in 1907, with the line being authorised on 7th April 1908. The next route to be built was that from Ardmillan Terrace to Slateford. There had been a proposal from the Colinton Tramways Company to build an electric tramway on private ground from Slateford to Colinton. In view of this, the proposal was to make the new route for electric traction. The line was built by the Council and leased to the Edinburgh and District Tramways Company. They opened it on 8th June 1910 using their cars numbered 28, 38, 64 and 74 that had been converted to electric operation from cable cars.

Another form of power was investigated by the Burgh Engineer when he visited Morecambe in 1911 to examine the petrol electric tramcars that the system had recently purchased. Though he recommended a trial with a petrol tramcar, nothing further came of it. Then there were thoughts of using trolleybuses. While nothing directly came of that, a review of possible tramway systems was undertaken in 1912. The running costs of the cable tramway were 9¼d per mile, compared to the neighbouring Leith Corporation's electric tramway that cost 4½d per mile. The report rejected the electric conduit and stud systems on the grounds of installation cost and safety. The recommended system was the overhead wire supply, except in Princes Street on aesthetic grounds. He also recommended motor buses for some routes. The Council pondered the report and decided, in 1913, to apply for an Act allowing them to run motorbuses. The Council reached an agreement with the Edinburgh and District Tramways Company where the Council would buy the vehicles and the Company would operate them. By this time the Council had decided to take over the operation of the tramways when the lease ran out in 1919.

The junction of Lothian Road and Princes Street. Tramcar number 223 appears to have a problem, with its driver peering down the slot at the cable. It has just approached a track point where the problem has occurred. The tramcar needs to ensure it releases one cable and picks up the correct cable after passing the point.

Events on the tramway were curtailed by the outbreak of war in 1914. Coal for the winding house boilers became scarce. Supplies of replacement parts became difficult, affecting maintenance of both cars and track. In 1915, much to the annoyance of the male employees, women conductors were employed. The Council looked into the possibility of purchasing the tramway prior to the end of the lease. They got advice that the offer price for the rolling stock and cable (the track and infrastructure were already owned by the Council) should be £25,000. The company wanted £75,000 but they agreed at £50,000. The transfer took place on 1st July 1919 with Stuart Pilcher as tramways Manager. The first action taken was to reduce the minimum fare from 1½d to 1d.

EDINBURGH CORPORATION CABLE TRAMWAYS 1919 – 1923

The first replacement of the cable tramways came in 1920, when it was clear that the original cable routes in the north of the city needed renewing. Rather than rebuild those cable tramway routes, the services were replaced by buses. Work also took place on converting other routes as well as the conversion of cable tramcars to electric operation and at the same time open-top cars were given covered roofs. The initial conversion meant putting up traction poles and the overhead supply, the cable conduit could stay in place as it would not interfere with electric operation. As the route to Pilrig met the Leith electric tramways it was an obvious choice for the first electric line to open. On 20th June 1922 it opened from Pilrig to Nether Liberton. In fact, the opening car (number 123) travelled from Leith onto Edinburgh rails at Pilrig and so to Nether Liberton, thus inaugurating the first electric conversion and through tramway route.

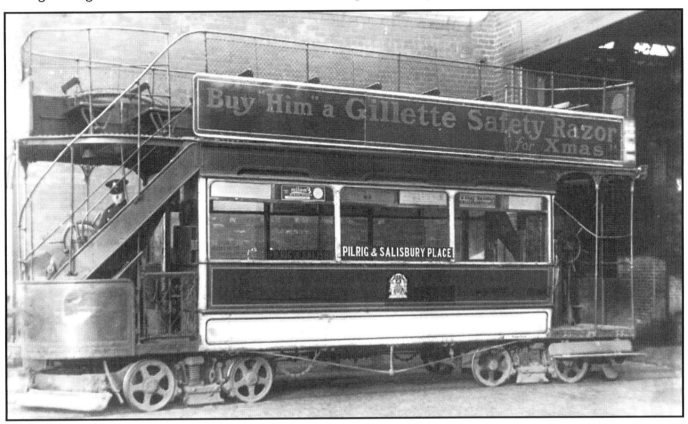

The Corporation crest on the side of this tramcar shows that the photograph was taken after it had taken over the running of the tramway in 1919, having purchased the tram fleet from the Edinburgh and District Tramways Company.

As each new conversion was opened the procedure was for a cable tram to be withdrawn as an electric car went into service until all the cable trams were in the depot. The Princes Street conversion was a little more contentious. As it was (and still is) the jewel of the city, there was great concern that putting overhead wires along it would spoil its beauty. So when it was time to convert the tramway along the road, Stuart Pilcher decided to do it all in one night. With a large gang of workmen and plenty of preparation, the work was started on the evening of Saturday 21st October 1922. As the cable trams were on their last runs the gang started erecting the centre traction poles into holes already prepared. The cable was removed from the conduit and the overhead wire attached to the traction poles. The exercise was complicated by the need to lay temporary tracks as the traction poles fouled one of the tracks in places. All was completed by 9.30am on Sunday morning when an electric tramcar was taken onto Princes Street and ran under its own power along the road. During the next two weeks the temporary tracks were replaced with permanent track. The temporary tracks were kept for other conversions around the city. Conversion continued and on Saturday evening 23rd June 1923, the last cable tramcar ran into the depot and so cable operation ceased in Edinburgh. It also saw the end of an exciting escapade of children. They would tie a piece of string onto a tin can and drop the string into the conduit slot. By jiggling the end of the string, it could be made to catch on the cable and be drawn along, bouncing its way down the street, much to the disapproval of policemen and tramways staff.

THE TRAMWAY FLEET

EDINBURGH NORTHERN CABLE TRAMWAYS COMPANY 1888 – 1896

Fleet number	Date built	Builder	Type	Number of seats
1 – 8	1887	Metropolitan Railway Carriage and Wagon Company Limited	Open top, bogie	32/20
9 – 16	1890/2	Falcon Engine and Car Works	Open top, bogie	22/18
17 – 18	1894/5	?	Single deck	26

Notes

All tramcars were transferred to Edinburgh and District Tramways on 31st December 1897 and renumbered 121 – 138.

Livery
Blue and cream.

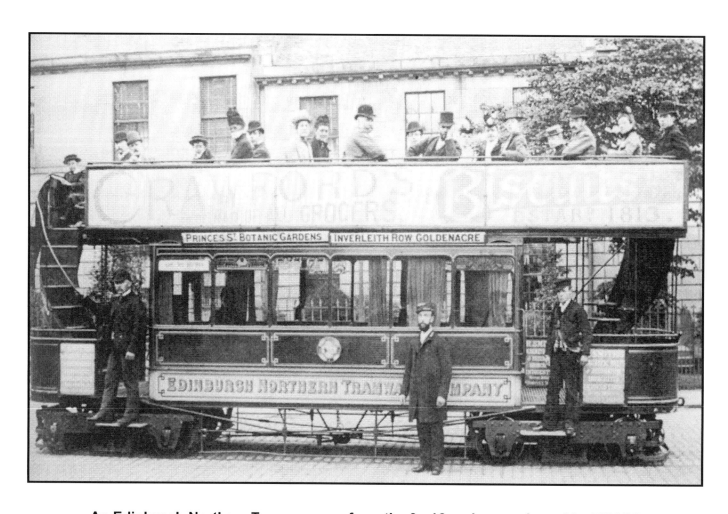

An Edinburgh Northern Tramways car from the 9 - 16 series purchased in 1890/92.

EDINBURGH AND DISTRICT TRAMWAYS COMPANY LIMITED 1896 – 1919

Fleet number	Date built	Builder	Type	Number of seats
112	1897	Edinburgh & District Tramway Co	Open top, bogie	28/18
121 – 128	1888/95	Metropolitan Railway Carriage and Wagon Company Limited	Open top, bogie	32/20
129 – 136	1890/92	Falcon Engine and Car Works	Open top, bogie	28/18
137 – 138	1894/95	?	Single deck	26
139 – 144	1897	G. F. Milnes & Co.	Open top, bogie	28/20
Note 1	1899/00	G. F. Milnes & Co.	Open top, bogie	28/20
Note 2	1899/01	Brown, Marshall & Co	Open top, bogie	28/20
209 – 228	1903	Electric Railway & Carriage Works Ltd	Open top, bogie	28/20
15, 17, 19, 53, 113	1906/08	Edinburgh & District Tramway Co	Open top, bogie Note 3	28/18
Note 4	1906/11	Edinburgh & District Tramway Co	Enclosed top, bogie	28/20

Notes

1 Numbers: 1, 26, 28, 30 – 40, 45, 46, 55, 62 – 65, 67, 68, 73, 74, 79, 81 – 83, 94, 103 – 105. All given an enclosed top 1908 – 1912, except 28, 38, 64 and 74.
2 Numbers: 2 – 4, 6, 8 – 12, 14, 16, 18, 20 - 24, 29 – 34, 36, 41 – 44, 56 – 58, 60, 61, 69 – 71, 77, 78, 80, 85, 88, 89, 91, 100, 101, 106, 107, 109, 111, 114 – 120, 137, 138, 145 – 169, 172 – 208. All given an enclosed top 1912.
3 All converted from horse cars.
4 Numbers: 5, 13, 25, 27, 35, 37, 47 – 52, 54, 59, 66, 72.

Livery
Madder and cream.

One of the first series of cars, now displaying the District Tramways name.

EDINBURGH CORPORATION CABLE TRAMWAYS 1919 – 1923

Fleet number	Date built	Builder	Type	Number of seats
1 – 6, 8 – 27, 29 – 37, 39 – 63, 65 – 73, 77 – 83, 85, 88 – 89, 91, 94, 100 – 101, 103 – 107, 109, 111 – 169, 172 – 228.	See above	Purchased from Edinburgh & District Tramway Co. see above	Open or enclosed top, bogie	28/20

Notes

Purchased from Edinburgh & District Tramway Co. see the table above.

The remaining tramcars were converted to electric operation soon after the system was taken over by the Council. When the cable tramway was converted to electric operation these cable tramcars were converted to electric power.

When the conversion to electric operation took place the cable tramcar fleet was redundant. Rather than losing these trams the Corporation undertook a conversion program and rebuilt most of them with electric motors. Here, number 215 shows the changes that were made including a four wheel chassis and a trolley pole.

REFERENCES

The System of Wire-Cable Railways for Cities and Towns, National Cable Railway Company, 1897

Edinburgh Northern Cable Tramway, The Engineer, 28th October 1887

Edinburgh Northern Cable Tramways, William Newby Colam, Proceedings of the Association of Municipal and Sanitary Engineers and Surveyors, Volume 17 1890/1

Tramways – Their Construction and Working, by D. Kinnear Clark, second edition 1894

Conversion of Edinburgh, Leith & Portobello horse tramways system into cable traction, by William Newby Colam, 1898

Transport World, Volume 18 - October 12, 1905 - page 369

Transport World, Volume 18 - November 9, 1905 - page 479

Scottish Tramway Fleets by Alan W. Brotchie, 1968, N. B. Traction

The Trams and Tramways in Scotland by Colin Hogarth, c1989, Carntyne House Publications

The Tramways of Eastern Scotland, by J. C. Gillham and R. J. S. Wiseman, 1991, Light Rail Transit Association

Edinburgh's Transport, The Early Years, by D. L. G. Hunter, 1992

Tram number 154 was built as an open-top car and was given a balcony top in 1912. It ran in this condition until the conversion to electric power in 1919 when it was rebuilt as a four-wheel car powered by electric motors.

CHAPTER 5

BIRMINGHAM CABLE TRAMWAYS

BIRMINGHAM CENTRAL TRAMWAYS COMPANY 1884 - 1896

The history of the development of tramways in Birmingham is complicated, with the Corporation interacting with a variety of different Companies, which themselves were taken over, amalgamated and/or newly created. In the early days of tramway transport, the trams in the city had most types of power sources. The operators used horse, steam, cable, accumulator and a little later trams powered from the overhead. Indeed, there was a period when all five forms were in use at the same time. This book is focussed on the cable tramway and so concentrates on those issues directly affecting that form of power.

In 1872 Birmingham Corporation obtained an Act to build a tramway from Colmore Row to Hockley Brook to link with the Birmingham and District Tramways Company tramway. Under the 1870 Tramway Act public bodies were prohibited from operating tramways. Therefore, the Corporation was obliged to lease the line to a private Company. Logically they entered into a contract with the Birmingham and District Tramway Company (BDTC) in order to allow a through service to be run from the city centre to Dudley Port and the first horse trams entered service in 1873. The BDTC had been formed as the result of the co-ordination of three separate, but similar, proposals. Unfortunately, the Company had financial troubles, resulting in most of its omnibus routes being closed by 1876, as was the tramway from Handsworth, New Inns and Dudley Port. The situation resulted in the establishment of a new organisation, the Birmingham Tramways and Omnibus Company (BT&OC), which also encompassed William Mayner's omnibus business. The Corporation built a line down the Bristol Road that was also leased to the Company. The new Company ran the system efficiently and over the next few years added to the omnibus side of the operation.

Cable tram number 84 in front of the old Snow Hill Station building. It was outside this building that Hallidie's Cable Railway Company demonstrated the cable system in 1883.

Cable tramcar number 79 made by the Falcon Engine and Car works in 1888 and part of the first batch of cars delivered to the Birmingham tramway. The photograph was taken after 20th April 1889 when the extension to the New Inns at Handsworth was opened.

The Birmingham Central Tramways Company Ltd. (BCTC) was founded in 1882 to operate 3 ft 6 in gauge steam tramways built by the city within its boundaries. As there was now a mix of gauges in the city, with the standard 4 ft 8½ in gauge and the narrow gauge at 3 ft 6 in. If both gauges were to be built in the same street a mixed gauge track would be required. This was discouraged by the Board of Trade so the Corporation warned the BCTC that when the lease came up for renewal in 1885 they would expect bids to incorporate a change to the narrow gauge. In 1883 the Patent Cable Tramway Company demonstrated their Hallidie cable tramway system in Birmingham and suggested to the Corporation that they could build their cable tramway by converting the Handsworth and Bristol Road routes to cable operation and changing the gauge to three feet six inches. The BCTC were concerned and began negotiations with the Patent Cable Tramway Company (PCTC), reaching an agreement where the PCTC would allow the BCTC to run the tramways under the new 1885 lease and in return they would use the PCTC patents. They passed all the tramway routes within the city boundary to the BCTC, leaving the BT&OC with two small routes outside the city. These were not viable and the BT&OC was sold to the BCTC in January 1886.

Edward Pritchard (who, with Joseph Kincaid of London) was Consulting Engineer to the Central Tramways Company. The two men visited America to see the cable tramways that had been opened. They came back enthused with the practicality of the system. It also gave them the opportunity to see the latest developments in the use of cable traction. The designs of the two Engineers were approved by the Borough Surveyor and the Public Works Committee. When the new lease started in 1885 the BCTC converted the standard gauge horse tramway from Colmore Row to Hockley Brook to the narrow gauge and cable operation, running a temporary horse bus service during the conversion.

In 1887 Andrew Hallidie visited Britain from the USA. During his stay he visited managers of those cable tramways in course of construction. He included the cable tramway nearly completed at Birmingham and the double track section that was about to be finished in Edinburgh, Scotland. No doubt he was able to pass on his experience and practical advice to the Engineers building those tramways.

The first section of the line, from Colmore Road to Hockley Brook, was 1⅔ miles long. It opened to the public on 24th March 1888. This was almost one month later than the opening of the first Edinburgh line and made it the third cable street tramway to open in Britain. The winding house and depot were located by the original terminus in Hockley. The second part of the tramway opened in 20th April 1889 and ran 1⅓ miles from Hockley Brook to the New Inns at Handsworth. The total length of the line was around 3 miles, mostly double track. The average steepest gradients were 1 in 20 to 1 in 13, and the sharpest curve about 45 ft. radius.

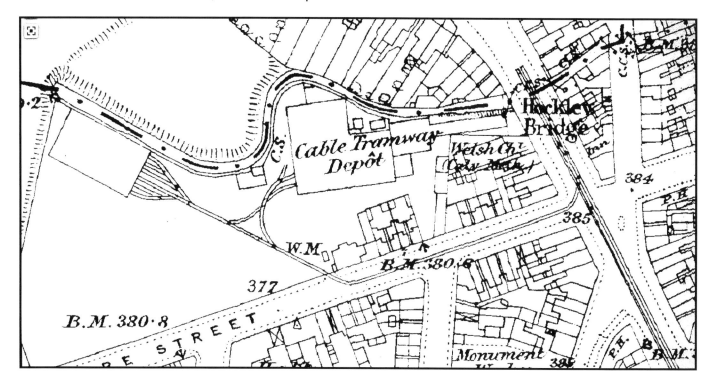

Above: The winding house and depot at Hockley Bridge. This map was made before the extension was built to the New Inns. The track in Whitmore Street, running up from the bottom left, and the depot area did not have a cable and a steam tram locomotive was used to move the cable cars in and out of the depot.

Below: Plan of the depot and winding house.

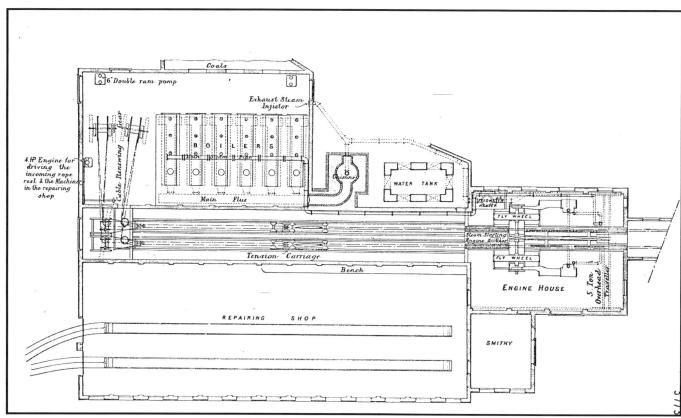

The furthest car, number 75, was the first to be delivered in 1888 from the Falcon Engine and Car Works while number 115 was also built by Falcon but in 1894.

The tramway was built by Jacob Bigg of Handsworth and the track was built on 'T' section steel bent and fabricated to form the yokes. It supported the slot rails and the running rails. A 3 ft 3 in deep and 3 ft wide ditch was dug to take the yokes which were set 4 ft apart. The slot rails were bolted to the yokes and then tie bars were bolted to the running rails, holding everything in position. In the construction of previous cable tramways the conduit and road were then built by placing formers through the yokes and pouring concrete around them However, a photograph of the construction of the Birmingham line appears to show a different sequence. The yokes had been put in place with the running rails, but the slot rails were not fixed at this stage. The concrete was poured to produce the conduit that supported the yokes; also making the access pits and fitting drainage pipes. Once the concrete had set the slot rails were bolted onto the yokes and the tie bars bolted between the slot and running rails. The final road surface was made up by stone sets placed on the concrete foundation.

Every seventh yoke also held a vertical pulley to carry the cable, with an access hatch for maintaining the pulley. In common with other cable tramways the pulleys were located to one side of the slot to reduce the amount of mud and dust falling onto the cable. The cable was 3⅜ in in circumference and was made of six strands, each strand of which was made from nineteen wires twisted together. The six strands were wound around a central hemp core. The arrangement gave a breaking strain of 33 tons. It was made by John and Edwin Wright of Birmingham. The Company estimated that the cable should last, with repairs, for a period of from twelve to eighteen months. At this rate the renewal costs would have been equivalent to about an eighth of a penny per car mile.

One particular issue regarding the cable was broken strands. On the Birmingham system broken strands were detected by arranging for the cable to pass through a hole in an iron plate that was slightly larger than the cable diameter. Any projecting strands striking these plates resulted in an electric bell ringing. The engineer noted the time of this signal, and knew when the damaged point of the cable would pass through the driving-house again. So he could arrange for its repair at the conclusion of the day's work. In case of any serious damage to the cable, the affected part was taken out and the cable re-spliced.

The winding house was located at Hockley Brook, roughly halfway along the route. The arrangement was different to the previous cable tramways built in Britain as, although the line was working as a single route, the tramway had two separate cables. One drove the Colmore Row to Hockley Brook section and the other from Hockley Brook to the New Inns at Handsworth. This arrangement enabled two particular advantages to be utilised. The first was that the City centre section was able to be opened nearly a year before the extension outside the City boundary. The second was that the speeds of the cables were different. The City section cable ran at 6mph while that outside the boundary, in Staffordshire, ran slightly faster at 8mph. The reason for this difference has not been found, but it was probably because the Act specified a maximum speed of 8mph but the Birmingham Corporation objected to such a high speed and insisted on it being lowered, while Handsworth Urban District were agreeable to the higher speed.

Inside the winding house were six boilers, from W. and J. Galloway and Sons, producing steam for the two Tangye 250 horse-power steam engines each driving a 15 ft diameter, 2 ft wide, flywheel that weighed eight tons. The gearing arrangement was such that either engine could drive both cables. The main driving wheels were different diameters, that for the Birmingham route was 10 ft while that for the Handsworth route was 13 ft 4 in diameter, giving the different cable speeds. There were two driving wheels for each cable and all had beechwood lining the grooves in order to minimise the danger of damaging the cable. Before going back to the track each cable passed over its own tensioning pulley, which was carried on its own wheeled frame pulled in tension by a five-ton weight.

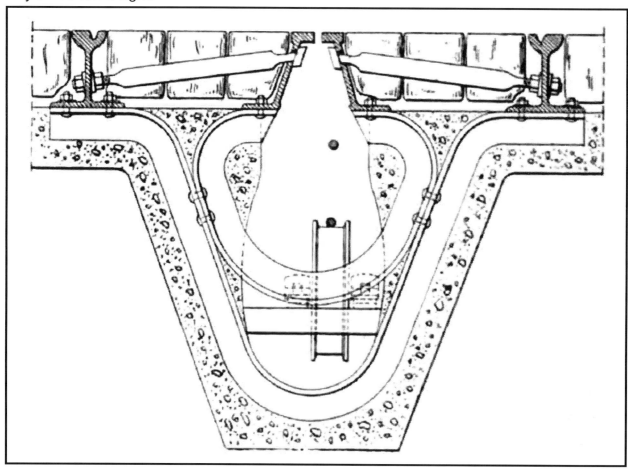

Cross-section and yoke of the track in Birmingham. The yoke was fabricated from 'T' section steel, with a pulley.

The tramcar shed was situated behind the winding house. A branch line was laid from the main line turning into Whitmore Street and then into the depot grounds. A six-road shed housed the fleet of tramcars and two separate sidings went into the back of the winding house to the repair shop. All the tracks from the start of Whitmore Street were fitted with a conduit, but had no cable. This meant that the tramcars could travel over the lines without having to remove their grips, but needed a different power source. The depot had its own shunter in the form of a steam tram locomotive, number 89, to facilitate movement of the tramcars.

There were no cables laid between the running line and the depot and workshops. To move the tramcars a steam tram locomotive, number 89 in the fleet, was allocated to the cable depot and shunted the tramcars in and out of the tram shed.

To run the tramway there were 32 tramcars. Initially, ten double-deck open-top tramcars were purchased from the Falcon Engine and Car Works, Loughborough, for the opening in 1888. When the extension to Handsworth was launched the following year, a further six cars were purchased, this time from a local Company, the Metropolitan Railway Carriage and Wagon Company Limited, from their factory at Saltley.

Number 78 from the first batch of ten cars delivered for the opening of the tramway in 1888.

The tramcars were fitted with a grip at each end. The grips were of the side entry type with idler wheels for allowing the cable to run smoothly through the grip when the tramcar was stationary. To move the tramcars, the driver would raise the grip jaws, clamping them together and allowing the cable to haul the car along. The driver would allow the cable to slip at the start in order to minimise jerking. The driver could also release the cable from the grip. This was necessary when the tramcar passed the winding house. The cables were diverted to the driving pulleys, so the driver would release the cable and coast across the section to reach the other cable where he would locate the cable and tighten the grip.

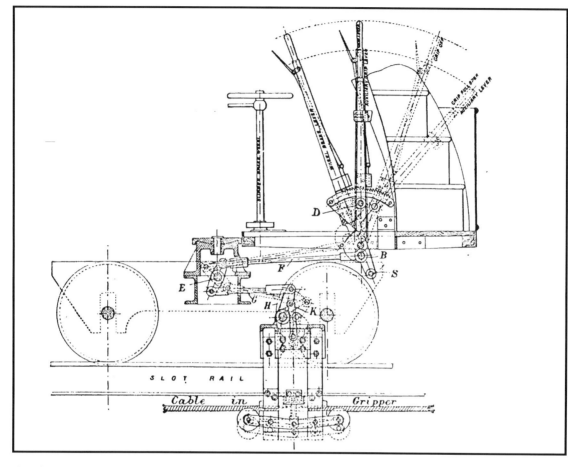

The grip used on the Birmingham cable tramway.

In the winding house were two large drums containing the spare cables. When it was necessary to replace the old cable, it would be cut and the new cable would be spliced to it. The engine would draw the old cable out while the new cable would be pulled into place. The final act was to cut the old cable off and splice the two ends of the new cable together. The staff soon had the opportunity to practice the procedure as, one afternoon a few weeks after the tramway opened to the public, a driver failed to release the grip at the winding house and the strain snapped the cable. The service on that section of the line halted and replacement of the cable was started. It took the staff all night to remove the old cable and replace it with the new cable and splice it. But by seven o'clock, the normal starting time, the tramway service was back in action.

Major General Hutchinson, Royal Engineers, from the Board of Trade, visited Birmingham on 24th March 1888 in order to inspect the system as part of the commissioning process. After the inspection the company held a luncheon. The chairman of the Company made a speech including the following words:

> "Practically this is the first application of the principle of cable traction in the suburbs of a great English town. How severe had been the strain of anxiety which the directors of the company had suffered in this matter could scarcely be expressed, but it was indeed satisfactory to consider that they had now to lean upon a calmer judgment and a wider experience than their own; and the approval of Major General Hutchinson convinced them that, unless difficulties should arise which no foresight could have prevented, the future of the Birmingham cable tramways would be a prosperous and a certain one. For that result he tendered the thanks of the company to the engineers."

Following the opening of the section from Colmore Road to Hockley Brook, the Company was able to concentrate on the final section of the line. This took just over a year and the extended line to the New Inns, Handsworth, was opened on 20th April 1889. The Company used the whole line to judge the profitability of cable traction. The usage of the tramway was encouraging. The Mechanical Traction Syndicate Ltd. in their 1896 book "The Cable System of Tramway Traction" reported that the passenger traffic on the route was very heavy compared with the Edinburgh Northern lines, with consequently greater profits. The book noted that the line contributed nearly half the profits of the BCTC. However, while the line proved profitable, it was not as much as was hoped. The results meant the company was not encouraged to convert the Bristol Road route to cable traction, given the significant initial investment required to convert the line. Instead the Company used accumulator-powered tramcars from 1890.

Tramcar number 94 was made by the Falcon Engine and Car Works and delivered in 1888, while number 95 was built by the Metropolitan Railway Carriage and Wagon Company Limited in 1889. It is not clear why the driver is moving from one car to the other.

A contemporaneous report said that the cable service was worked by sixteen cars on all the days of the week except Saturday, when two extra cars were added to the service. All the cars were on the road for an average of sixteen hours a day, but relief was given to the drivers and conductors for periods varying from two and a half to three and a half hours. Crew meals had to be taken while travelling, except when the mealtime occurred during a man's rest period. Men were expected to be at the depot fifteen minutes before starting in the morning and the conductors were occupied from ten to twenty minutes at night in getting their accounts squared by a clerk. Each man worked more than thirteen hours a day for the whole week.

A conductor's wages for the first two years were 3s. 6d.; after two years, if no complaints had been made against them, they were entitled to 3d. a day more; after three years' service a conductors' wages were 4s. a day. Drivers pay began at 4s. 6d a day, and after six months' service rose to 5s. a day, and after one year's service to 5s. 6d. a day. In 1896 Consul Jarrett from the USA paid a visit to Britain, including a trip to the city. In the report of his experiences his comments on the Birmingham tramway was *"The cars on all the tramways are long, narrow, double-decked, ugly, and dirty affairs, having no kind of conveniences or provisions for the comfort of the traveling public. No American city would tolerate such hideous things."*

Now there must be a slight digression from the cable story. With profits that disappointed the Company, the decision was made to run the Bristol route using accumulator trams. The track had to be changed, both to bring the gauge in line with the 3 ft 6 in used by all the other tramways in the city and strengthening the track to take the heavier double-deck bogie tramcars. The accumulator route started running in 1890 and the Company soon discovered the problems of using accumulators. The batteries were stored under the passenger seats and, before long, passengers were complaining that the acid fumes were being released into the saloon. Then it was found that the battery cases were being eroded by the acid and they began leaking, damaging passengers' clothing. In 1892 the batteries were replaced by new Epstein Electric Accumulator Company products. Initially this seemed to resolve the problems but after around a year the same issues came back. The costs of running the route became so high that the Company was losing significant amounts, such that the whole organisation was in debt. In nearby Walsall the South Staffordshire Tramway Company had recently installed an overhead electric tramway. The BCTC applied to the Corporation to install an overhead supply. The Corporation objected as it was thought that the overhead wiring would be unsightly. This decision meant that the Company continued to lose money and soon had severe financial problems.

The steam engine and winding pulleys. The depot and winding house were located at Hockley and it drove two cables, one to Snow Hill Railway Station and the other outside the city boundary to Handsworth.

CITY OF BIRMINGHAM TRAMWAYS COMPANY

A Scottish civil engineer who had developed his career in Canada, James Leveson Ross, was President and Vice-President of the Toronto and Montreal Street Railway Companies and the major shareholder in the Canadian Pacific Railway, and Sir William Mackenzie, a Canadian businessman, entered the scene. How or why they became involved is not known. They established the City of Birmingham Tramways Company (CBT) in 1896 with the intention of taking over the BCTC. Their background was experience in the electrification of street railways in Canada and they went on to persuade the Birmingham Corporation to agree to overhead electrification, though not until 1901.

The CBT acquired the assets of the BCTC on 29th September 1896. They recognised the financial strength of the cable route and were happy to concentrate their efforts on electrifying the accumulator and horse routes. Indeed, the Company purchased a further six open-top tramcars in 1898, from the Metropolitan Railway Carriage and Wagon Company Limited, to support the existing cable fleet. In 1901 ten more tramcars were built by the Company. They were single-deck, bogie, cross bench tramcars. Quite what the rationale was behind this decision is not known. This design of tramcar body is more associated with sunshine and seaside holiday towns, two things Birmingham could not claim. It soon became clear that the cars were unsuitable for the route and an alternative future was sought. Two of them were given electric motors and used on the Lichfield Road route under the low bridge at Aston Station. When the bridge was reconstructed in 1906 they were no longer required. They joined the other four cars (also converted to electric operation) on the Kinver line, where they probably were only used on excursions and public holidays, when every tramcar was put in use. The CBT replaced these cars in 1902 by six open-top, bogie cars that worked on the route until its conversion to electric power. In the same year the CBT became a subsidiary of the British Electric Traction Company Limited (BET).

Above: Tramcar number 123 was purchased from the Metropolitan Railway Carriage and Wagon Company Limited in 1898. It carries the City of Birmingham Tramways Company initials.

Below: The BET took over the CBTC in 1902 and the tramcars were given the familiar magnet and wheel BET logo.

In 1909 the Handsworth Council purchased the cable tramway within their boundary, from Hockley to the New Inns, Handsworth and immediately leased it to the CBT to carry on running the line. The Birmingham Corporation had for some years been wanting to take on the operation of the tramways that they owned and leased to BCTC, as and when the leases expired. The cable tramway lease ran for a further nine years, expiring on 30th June 1911. When the lease expired the Corporation took over the route. Handsworth Council took over the cable tramway in its area. In November 1911 the Handsworth Urban District Council was absorbed by the City of Birmingham and Birmingham tramcars ran through Handsworth. During the last few months of the cable tramway operation, the Corporation erected an overhead power supply along the route. The intention was for the cable trams to be withdrawn on 30th June and the Corporation electric tramcars to start in 1st July. The Corporation had been unable to rebuild the track while the cable trams were running and so initially the electric tramcars ran over the cable tracks, complete with their conduit. The changes on the track were carried out in the latter part of 1912 and cable-operated public transport ended in Birmingham until 2003 when a Doppelmayr Cable Car people mover was opened linking Birmingham International Station with the airport.

One of the ten single-deck, crossbench cars purchased from G. C. Milnes, Voss and Company, numbers 141—150 in 1901. Unsurprisingly, they were not popular and two were transferred to the Aston Cross to Gravelly Hill route and converted to electric operation. Later that year they and four other single-deck cars (also converted for electric operation) were transferred to the Kinver Light Railway (KLR), probably for use at bank holidays. On the KLR they were renumbered 63—68.

THE TRAMWAY FLEET

BIRMINGHAM CENTRAL TRAMWAYS 1884 – 1896

Fleet number	Date built	Builder	Type	Number of seats
75 – 94	1888	Falcon Engine and Car Works	Open top, bogie	24/20
95 – 100	1889	Metropolitan Railway Carriage and Wagon Company Limited	Open top, bogie	24/20
113 – 118	1894/5	Falcon Engine and Car Works	Open top, bogie	24/20

Notes

All transferred to City of Birmingham Tramways 15th October 1896

Livery
Crimson and cream.

The preserved City of Birmingham cable tramcar when it was stored at the Black Country Living Museum. It has since been moved to the Crich Tramway Museum collection and is currently awaiting restoration and is not on public display.

CITY OF BIRMINGHAM TRAMWAYS COMPANY 1896 – 1911

Fleet number	Date built	Builder	Type	Number of seats
75 – 94	1888	Falcon Engine and Car Works	Open top, bogie	24/20
95 – 100	1889	Metropolitan Railway Carriage and Wagon Company Limited	Open top, bogie	24/20
113 – 118	1894/5	Falcon Engine and Car Works	Open top, bogie	24/20
119 – 124	1898	Metropolitan Railway Carriage and Wagon Company Limited ‡	Open top, bogie	24/20
141 – 150	1901	G. C. Milnes, Voss & Co.	Single deck, Crossbench †	40
172 – 177	1902	United Electric Car Co.	Open top, bogie	24/20

Notes

‡ One of the series was sold to the Matlock Tramways Company where it was cut down to single deck.

† Two of the 141-150 series were converted to electric operation in 1904 for the Aston Cross to Gravelly Hill route then transferred the same year with four others (also converted) to Kinver Light Railway and renumbered 63 – 68.

One cable tramcar has survived. It has not been possible to identify its fleet number. It has the design characteristic of the 75 – 100 design, though was found carrying a maker's plate from the Midland Railway Carriage & Wagon Works, which is at odds with the records. It had been sold when the tramway was converted to electric operation, to become a summerhouse in a Smethwick garden. It was discovered and rescued by the Black Country Museum Transport Group and was acquired and moved to the Museum in the early 1970s. In need of restoration the remains of the body were stored in the open with the intention to undertake restoration. This did not materialise and in 2016 it was donated to the National Tramway Museum, Crich, as they had no example of a cable tramcar nor of any tram from the West Midlands. It is in store awaiting restoration.

Livery
Sage green and cream.

REFERENCES

Tramways – Their Construction and Working, by D. Kinnear Clark, second edition 1894
Street Railway Gazette – February 1887
Street Railway Gazette – December 1887
Street Railway Gazette – January 1888
Street Railway Gazette – April 1888
The Engineer – 22nd June 1888
The Engineer – 29th June 1888
United States Congressional Serial Set, Report by Consul Jarrett, 1892 by United States Government Printing Office
Birmingham Before the Electric Tram, by David Harvey, 2013, Amberley Publishing

CHAPTER 6

LONDON

BRIXTON HILL CABLE TRAMWAY 1892 - 1904

LONDON TRAMWAYS COMPANY

The London Tramways Company (formerly the Metropolitan Street Tramways Company) had built horse tramways to serve much of south London. One line went from Blackfriars Bridge to a terminus at the bottom of Brixton Hill, by Water Lane. The Company was keen to extend the line to Streatham, but realised that the steep Brixton Hill would both require many extra horses to pull the tramcars up the hill and that they would only be able to travel very slowly. In 1888 an alternative solution was sought. No doubt the Directors were aware of the cable tramway that had been opened at Highgate in 1884. They applied to Parliament with the London Tramways Company (Extension) Act 1889 for authority to build a one and a half mile long tramway from the horse car terminus at Water Lane to Telford Avenue, Streatham, where a depot would be built. In the following year they applied for further authority to use cable traction on the line and to convert the horse tramway from Water Lane to Kennington to cable operation, an additional one and a quarter miles.

Outside the small overnight depot at Brixton, a dummy cable car uncouples from the horse tramcar that it has just brought down Brixton Hill. For the next part of its journey to Blackfriars a horse has been harnessed to the tram. This arrangement meant that passengers could stay on the tramcar and did not have to change cars.

The consulting engineer was William Newby Colam, who worked closely with the contractors Dick, Kerr & Company Limited and their engineer James More. All had experience of building cable tramways in Britain. The initial route length, from Telford Road to Kennington, was two and three-quarter miles with a steepest incline of 1 in 20. Track laying began with digging a ditch for the cable conduit and the foundation for the rails. Beneath the conduit were the drainage pipes and a foundation laid for the yokes and running rails. Short yokes were laid at 3 ft 7 in centres along the route. The running rails were laid with tie bars connecting the rails to the yokes, then the slot rails were bolted in place. The conduit (19 in deep and 9 in wide) was made using wooden formers and pouring concrete around them. Vertical pulleys were fitted every 50 ft, each with an access hatch for maintenance. At the termini there were access hatches to allow grips to be removed and the terminal pulleys to be maintained. On curves, horizontal pulleys were set as close as required to guide the cable around the arc. The road surface was finished with granite setts.

Two tramcars pass on the Brixton Hill tramway. The dummy towing cars hauled the horse tramcars the 2½ miles between Streatham Hill and Kennington from 1892. This was later extended ¾ mile from Streatham Hill to Streatham Village in 1896.

The cable was 3⅝ in in circumference and consisted of six strands, each of seven wires, wound around a Manilla hemp rope core with a breaking strain of 40 tons. It was made by George Craddock and Company of Wakefield and weighed 30 tons. The support pulleys were fitted to carry the cable 1 in to the side of the slot, giving some protection from falling dirt and muck.

The winding house and depot were built in Streatham, opposite Telford Avenue. The four boilers were manufactured by Babcock and Wilcox and only three were required to fuel the steam engines, the fourth was available as a spare. There were two steam engines, only one being needed to run the tramway, so there was always a spare. Either could be connected to the 11 ft diameter grip pulley. The groove of the main pulley was lined with white metal segments to give a good grip on the cable. Before passing out of the winding house the cable was looped around a tension pulley. This was mounted on a wheeled frame that was held in tension using a counter weight. The speed of the cable (and the speed of the subsequent cable for the extension) was 8 mph. Under the track outside the winding house were the pulleys directing the cables to and from the engines. They were located in a pit 81 ft long and 12 ft wide with an access tunnel from the winding house.

The depot was rather unusual as the entrance was significantly lower than the storage roads. There was a long ramp leading up from the entry to the main depot to a traverser, located about three-quarters of the way towards the back of the shed. Here the horse tramcars would be moved to an appropriate siding. The depot tracks were equipped with cable drives, limited to 2½ mph. There was another small depot at Brixton Road, where a passenger car and dummy were stored

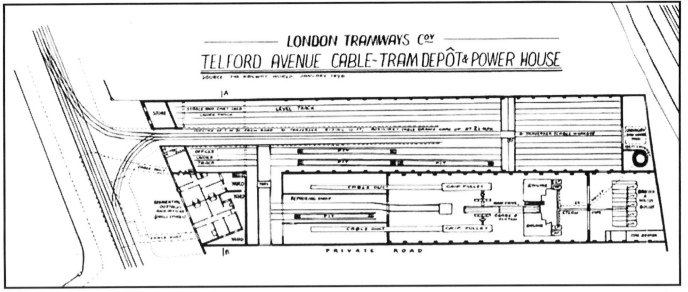

The engine house and tramcar sheds at Telford Avenue. Access was by a slope up the middle of the storage roads to a traverser.

The entrance to the tramcar depot at Telford Avenue. The single track led up the slope to a traverser giving access to all the storage tracks. Horse tram trailers can be seen above the access track.

overnight to be ready for an early start.

An early decision had been to use separate dummy cars to haul horse tramcars over the line. This enabled the passengers to remain on their horse tramcar for the whole of the journey, both on and off the cable section. Unlike the dummies used in San Francisco and Highgate Hill, there was no seating for passengers. The dummy cars were small four-wheel vehicles that carried a driver and the grip mechanism and brakes. Initially there were 30, later a further 12 were added. Each was fitted with a coupling at both ends, as were the horse tramcar trailers. The grip was operated using a handwheel mounted on a screw shaft. There were two sets of side entry jaws, one either side of the central grip. The driver would engage the cable and tighten the jaws to propel the car. In cases of emergency or maintenance, the lower section of the grip could be unbolted and removed either in the depot or at one of the maintenance hatchways along the track. There was a lever-operated handbrake operating on all four wheels, while a second lever was linked by wires to the brakes on the trailer to enable all eight wheels of the dummy and trailer to be operated by the driver.

The planned extension of the line southward from Telford Avenue to the centre of Streatham Village, by the Tate Library, was opened in 1895, adding a further ¾ mile to the route. The new section was driven from the winding house by a second cable. The road by the winding house was marked to show drivers where they were required to disconnect the grip from the cable and coast past the place where the cable turned to the winding drums and then pick up the second cable for the final part of the journey.

The section of the line from Telford Avenue to Water Lane, Kennington was the first to be built. It was inspected on 11th August 1891, by Major General Hutchinson for the board of Trade who passed it as suitable for use only by horse trams (subject to review when the change to cable operation was extended to Kennington). A service was begun, but with all the problems that the cable line was meant to resolve. It was only when the final part of the route was completed and the cable installed, that Major General Hutchinson inspected the whole line on 7th December 1892 and authorised the use of cable traction. The system had its first big problem just six days later when a strand of the cable snapped causing damage to pulleys. The cable was stopped and rather than replace that section of cable it was decided to replace the whole cable with a spare. A horse tram service was put in place while the new cable was fitted. This took a day, but the Board of Trade insisted on another inspection before cable working could restart. It was a week before the inspection took place and cable working was again authorised.

One of the main steam engines available to drive the cable drums. Either of the two engines could be used to power the whole system, keeping the other as a reserve. Beyond the wall on the right was the tramcar depot.

The extension from Telford Avenue to Streatham Village, and the Tate Library, was built and opened on January 1896 making the line 2¾ miles long, then the longest cable tramway in the country. It was to become a very busy part of the London Tramways Company network carrying an eighth of all the LTC passengers. There were 67 tramcars used on the route, though there is no record of which particular horse cars were used on the cable car route. The 44-seat passenger tramcars were fitted with a special lighting system for the passengers. Horse tramcars were usually fitted with a small oil lamp on each bulkhead, giving a faint light at night. Those used on the cable route were fitted with batteries that lit bulbs in the saloon. The batteries were recharged in the depot. Soon after the extension was opened the Board of Trade objected to the horse trams as they had an access step on the front nearside of their platforms. The opportunity was taken to make a further modification when making the change. The side of the car was lengthened with an extra window, while keeping the overall length at 22 ft. To do this the existing bulkheads, that were set at right angles to the sides, were removed and new bulkheads were fitted at an angle. This enabled the bench seats to be extended to take an extra passenger per side, raising the seating to 46 per car. These are possibly the only tramcars in the British Isles to have such angled bulkheads.

The early tramcars had eight windows and bulkheads at right-angles to the sides. They also had a step and entrance on both sides of the two platforms. The Board of Trade objected to this and the tramcars were modified.

The tramcars were modified to take the gripper mechanism, thus eliminating the need for the dummy cars. They also had the saloon sides extended by one window and an angled bulkhead, that gave extra seating in the saloon and removed the near-side platform step and entrance.

A further modification came in 1898 when some of the horse tramcars were modified. George Woolley, the Superintendent of Works of the Company, designed a removable grip that could be fitted to a modified horse tramcar. Operating rods were fitted to each end of the tramcar with a fixing frame at one end. The grip was a mechanism that had a small frame above the slot with a plate extending into the conduit to the jaws of the grip. This was separate from the tramcar. The grip could be attached and detached at each end of the cable tramway. Two men were required to place the grip under the car and bolt it in place. At the other end of the cable tramway, that grip would be removed ready to be attached to another tram. This had the advantage of no longer requiring the dummy car and its driver, making a useful saving. However, the London Tramways Company was not going to be able to continue running the line.

A poor but rare photograph, after the horse trams were converted to cable operation they were required to pick-up and drop off the grip at Kennington. The tramcars were fitted with the necessary levers and links reaching below the platform floor. Here a mechanic slides the grip to the tramcar. It fitted below the platform and was bolted to the levers. The tramcar could then be drawn up the hill by cable. On the left a car that had just arrived from travelling down the hill has a horse attached for the remainder of the journey to Blackfriars bridge.

LONDON COUNTY COUNCIL

By the 1890s the LCC had decided to take on the operation of all tramways within London. However, things did not always go smoothly. The first opportunity to compulsorily purchase the LTC came in 1892, but the LCC lost the chance, so they tried at the next opportunity, a two-mile section at Newington Butts. The negotiations went badly and the Board of Trade appointed an arbitrator. The LTC objected to the valuation and took the matter to court. It lost the case and, seeing the way things were going, decided to negotiate a sale of its whole network to the LCC. This included the cable tramway and this passed into LCC ownership with the rest of the Company on 1st January 1899.

The LCC took over operating the tramway in 1899 and, although immediately intending to convert the line to electric traction, did proclaim their ownership of the tramcars by displaying "L. C. C." on each side. In fact the cable trams ran under their management for four years.

Almost mirroring the events of 1892 soon after the cable tramway had opened, later in 1899 the system had a cable break. Though they worked all night the system was still being repaired the next morning and in order to give the public a tramway service they resorted to horse power until the cable could be returned to service.

When the LCC took over it was clear that the future for tramways was electric power. Being London, the authorities decided that they did not want overhead wires spoiling the ambience of their streets. They chose to install the conduit method of power supply, so electrifying the old horse tramways became a priority for the LCC. The horse lines either side of the cable section were electrified, but of course the electric trams could not run on the cable tramway. This meant that passengers travelling from Westminster had to change to a cable tramcar at Kennington. But this was not to last long as the cable line was closed on 5th April 1904 for conversion to electric power. Part of the conversion meant that the steam engines were connected to generators to produce electricity for the tramway.

In 1902 the Reverend John P. Hobson had a trip on the cable tramway and wrote about it in "The Leisure Hour" in 1902-1903 (an illustrated weekly magazine for home published by the Religious Tract Society). His essay is interesting as it gives the reaction of an ordinary passenger. He starts:-

> "Anyone who travels by the tramcars from Blackfriars or Westminster Bridge to Streatham has noticed that soon after passing Kennington Gate and entering upon the Brixton Road a longer pause than usual is made. The horses are taken out, and a machine is run under the car with a sudden jerk. Shortly afterwards the car proceeds upon its way without any visible means of locomotion. The "machine" is a gripper which is fastened beneath the car and grips a cable by which you are carried along."

On the return journey he stopped at the winding house:-

"Soon we are gliding quickly down the hill, which tests the strength of the brakes of the car. Here we are again at the working-station. Let us get down. We are armed with an order which Mr. Baker, the courteous manager of the London County Council Tramways Department, has given me, and so we can walk in. We mount the slope, up and down which the cars are run by a special cable. We are met by the engineer, who is good enough to show us over. We arrive at the shed where about twenty cars are standing ready to be used. At the end of the shed is a platform on to which the cars are run, and then by means of a mechanical lift are raised to a floor above, where a further supply of cars can be stored. At this depot thirty-nine cars are kept, twenty-eight are stored elsewhere, so that when in full work sixty-seven cars are on the line running from Streatham to London. In the busy part of the day the service to any one of the three London termini, i.e. Westminster, Blackfriars, or Lord Wellington, is every two minutes, at other times three minutes. The cars run in the following order: yellow to Lord Wellington, blue to Blackfriars, red to Westminster. They carry forty-four or forty-eight persons each, according as they are built on the old or new pattern. The latter have the end walls placed diagonally to the sides, and so get much more platform

The entrance to Telford Avenue tramcar depot (the entrance on the left) with the winding house on the right.

space and greater seating room. It will thus be seen that 3000 passengers could be carried at one time all the way. As the car takes about two hours to go to its destination and back, and runs for about sixteen hours, the total number of passengers would be 24,000 if the cars were always full and if the passengers travelled all the way. The number getting in and out on the journey far exceeds the empty places, so that the actual number travelling is about 37,000 a day or 13,500,000 in the year. Our guide takes us to the engine-room, where four double-furnace water-tube boilers are placed, three of which are at work producing steam to drive the engines in the shed hard by. Light and spacious this is. In the centre revolve the enormous wheels which carry the power to the steel ropes. The wheels are worked by an engine of 600 horse-power. Another engine of the same power stands idle on the other side of the shed ready for use. On the left of the building, running over several wheels, is the London cable. It is 30,000 feet long, 1 1/8 inch in diameter, and weighs five tons to the mile. It takes forty minutes to accomplish its journey to Kennington and back, or, in other words, its speed is eight miles an hour. The cables run in a conduit about two feet deep made under the two lines."

"When going on the straight they pass over vertical pulleys or sheaves twelve inches in diameter, and about fifty feet apart. When turning curves they run round horizontal pulleys of the same diameter, and at intervals in proportion to the curves. Near this cable stands a second ready for use if the other should break. The life of a cable varies, sometimes its work is over in eighteen months. One cable lasted as long as two years and five months. This one rope must have hauled some 24,500,000 passengers. The chief danger is that a strand of the rope breaks, the gripper through which it passes then causing it to pucker up, and soon, of course, the car comes to a standstill. What happens is similar to the unravelling of a piece of string, with a result that the tube gets choked up by the unravelled portion being carried forward by the gripper. The replacing of an old cable is effected in a very simple manner. The old rope is cut; the new one is spliced to it, and for the last time the old one goes on its journey, dragging its successor after it. When the end of the new cable appears it is spliced on to the other end, and thus takes up its burden of work in place of the old one which has been run off on to a drum. This change is effected in a night. It is not always necessary to replace the whole of a cable when the damaged or worn portion is only small; the damaged portion is cut out, and a piece of spare cable is spliced in its place. The Streatham cable is of the same thickness as the London cable, but is only about 10,000 feet in length. The total length of the two cables is seven and a half miles, and they weigh forty tons. Near where the London cable finds its way out into the street is an ingenious arrangement to regulate the pressure on the rope. It consists of a weight equal to four tons attached to one of the wheels over which the rope runs, and it keeps that rope taut, and thus counterbalances any slackness there may be upon the rope at any given time, by reason of fewer cars happening to be upon it. "Would you like to go below? " asks our guide. "Yes, certainly, we should like to see all there is to see." So we descend some steps. "Take care, stoop." You are passing under the Streatham cable, and it runs close beside you as you walk along a narrow passage. You turn aside under one or two arches, and arrive at the pit built under the road in front of the working-station. This pit is eighty-one feet long, twelve feet broad, and eight feet high. It is lit with electricity. In it are large pulleys about twenty-eight feet in periphery, or 9.3 in diameter, which carry the ropes round into the road to begin their work. As the grippers have here to be transferred from one cable to the other, the cables overlap for a short distance. The London rope runs round a wheel at the south end of the pit, while the Streatham runs over a wheel at the north end. When a car arrives at this point it stops. The gripper is opened, and the rope hitherto used is released and the other one is pulled up into the place it occupied, and the car goes on its way. We could see this process at work from underneath, the car being directly over our heads. "We will now turn back; but be careful, for if you touched the rope running so steadily by you, you would receive a terrible wound."

"At the gate we saw one of the grippers lying against the wall. The gripper when at work runs in the slot which extends the whole length of the line. The part above ground consists of a carriage which is thrust beneath the car, and fits under its centre, together with a long arm which is attached to the platform of the car, and is worked by a wheel. When the wheel is turned one way the jaws of the gripper are opened downwards, leaving a space of two inches, into which the rope is drawn. By moving it the other way the driver tightens the gripper upon the rope, and so the car is drawn smoothly on. Sometimes a second or two elapses before the rope is actually gripped, and the racing of the rope through the gripper causes a vibration which is very noticeable. The employment of these grippers in place of the old gripper cars which, fastened to the front of the cars, dragged them along, has had the effect of reducing the rolling-stock by one half, and in consequence has reduced the straining upon the rope, and the amount of wear and tear upon the permanent way."

THE CABLE TRAMWAY FLEET

LONDON TRAMWAYS COMPANY 1892 - 1899

Fleet number	Date built	Builder	Type	Number of seats
1 – 30	1892	Unknown	Dummy	Nil
31 – 42	c1895	Unknown	Dummy	Nil
67 Total	?	Unknown	Open top, horse tramcars	44†

Notes

All transferred to London County Council 1st January 1899

† Rebuilt around 1897 from seven windows to eight, increasing the seating to 46 and adding grip equipment.

Livery
Not known.

The tramcar depot at Telford Avenue showing the access ramp leading to a traverser. The tracks on the right are equipped with maintenance pits.

LONDON COUNTY COUNCIL 1899 - 1904

Fleet number	Date built	Builder	Type	Number of seats
1 – 30	1892	Unknown	Dummy	Nil
31 – 42	c1895	Unknown	Dummy	Nil
67 Total	?	Unknown	Open top, horse tramcars	44

Notes

All transferred from the London Tramways Company 1st January 1899

REFERENCES

Tramways – Their Construction and Working, by D. Kinnear Clark, Second Edition 1894
A Chat on a Cable Car, by Rev. John P. Hobson, 1902, published in The Leisure Hour
A History of London Transport Volume 1, by T. C. Barker and Michael Robbins, 1963, Published by George Allen and Unwin
London County Council Tramways, Volume 1 South London, by E. R. Oakley, 1989, Published by London Tramways History Group
How the Trams Came to Streatham, by Brian Bloice, Streatham Society News, No 215, Winter 2013/14

A pair of horses stand by at Kennington, ready to take over the tramcar from the dummy car. The arrangement meant that passengers could remain on the tram. After the London County Council took over the running of the tramway there was a short period when the line either side of the cable section had been electrified. This meant that the passengers had to change tramcars in order to travel up or down Brixton Hill.

CHAPTER 7

MATLOCK CABLE TRAMWAY 1892 - 1904

MATLOCK TRAMWAY COMPANY LIMITED 1892—1898

Warm springs were discovered in Matlock Bath in the 1690s and the town became known for the curative nature of the waters. Visitor numbers increased and the town received royal approval with the visit in 1832 of Princess Victoria of Kent (to become Queen Victoria). However, there was a disadvantage for the visitor taking the waters. The many hydropathic hotels were on Matlock Bank, up a steep slope from Matlock Bridge, the river and the main road to the town. Inevitably most of the visitors staying at the hotels were there to cure medical complaints. For them the half-mile walk up the steep hill (with a rise of 300 feet) was difficult if not impractical. Local transport was available, but at a price. In the 1870s the Smedley Hydro Hotel offered to take visitors from Matlock Bridge Station to the hotel for 6d (around £12 in today's money).

The report of the inaugural ceremony of the cable tramway, written contemporaneously with the opening of the line, gave a short background history of the tramway. It stated that a local citizen, Job Smith, was travelling in San Francisco from 1863 to 1868 when he saw the new cable tramway in the town. He recognised this as a possible way of providing passenger travel in Matlock. He wrote to a friend, John Smedley, suggesting this as a solution for his home town. Smedley was unable to take the idea any further and Smith promised himself to pursue this when he got back home. This he did in 1868. There is a major flaw in this version of events. The inventor of the world's first street cable tramway, Andrew Smith Hallidie, tells us that he first thought about using cable traction in the streets of San Francisco in 1869 and the line, the Clay Street route, was built in 1873. By the time the line opened, Smith had been away from America for five years. So quite what prompted his thoughts to a street cable tramway for Matlock is unknown. It would seem that Smith was very proud of his visit to America as in his photographs he always wore an American Western style hat.

Tramcar number 2 waits at the lower terminus at Crown Square, Matlock Bridge.
The photograph shows nearly the whole route going up the hill .

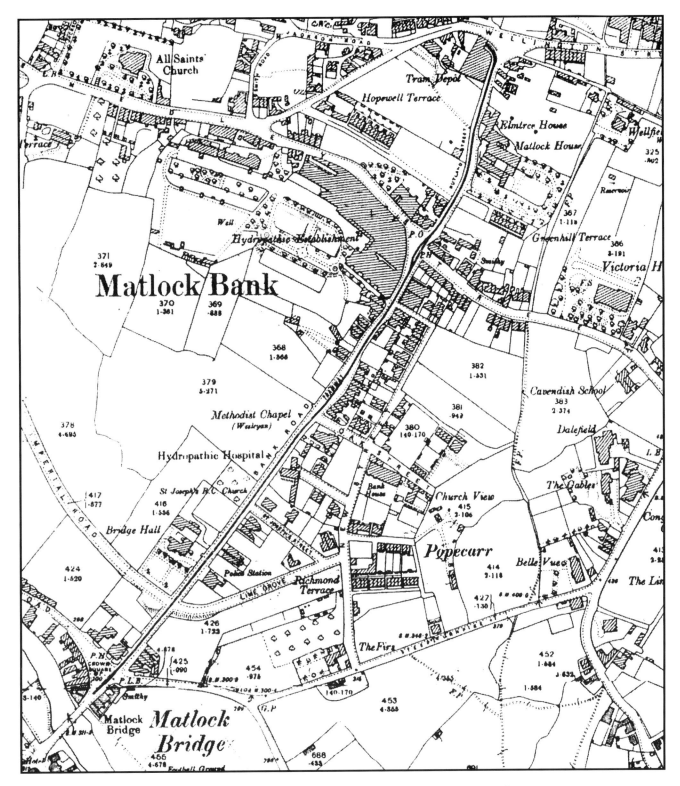

Map of the Matlock cable tramway from the 1897 Ordnance Survey map.

The first four cable tramways in Britain opened in 1884 (Highgate Hill), 1888 (Edinburgh and Birmingham) and 1891 (Brixton Hill). Hearing about these and the line in San Francisco may have influenced him. At some stage Smith started making moves towards developing a cable tramway. He contacted local businessmen, who showed interest. His scheme was to lay a line along Bank Road and into Rutland Street, up the side of the hill to Matlock Bank and the hydro hotels. The Council pointed out that Rutland Street was too narrow to accommodate a street tramway. This brought plans to a halt. Smith focussed on the subject again when, in 1890, he read a report on the Lynton and Lynmouth Cliff Railway. By this time Rutland Street had been widened. He was a member of the local Council and he raised the idea at a meeting. However, the Council did not want the responsibility of building such a line. So Smith started approaching entrepreneurs to see if he could raise enough backing to privately construct the line.

George Croydon Marks, who at the time was engineer of the Lynton and Lynmouth Cliff Railway, read a report of one of Smith's speeches and he drew the attention of George Newnes (the publisher and native of Matlock Bath) to the idea of a cable tramway in Matlock. Newnes wrote to Smith suggesting that he was ideal to take forward the project with all his experience of cable tramways. The outcome was that Croydon Marks was commissioned to undertake a survey for such a line. It was to run from Crown Square, up Bank Road, then up Rutland Street terminating at the corner of Wellington Street. As a result Newnes offered to fund the building of the line. It was felt that it would be more acceptable if local people were party to the line and so an advertisement was placed in a local newspaper asking for applications for shares, but only from "ratepayers of the Parish of Matlock", and a new Company was formed. Initially it was proposed to build the winding house at Matlock Bridge, at the bottom of the hill. But it was pointed out that this area was prone to flooding from the River Derwent and this might extinguish the boiler fires. So the plan was changed and a site for a winding house was sought near the top of the hill on Rutland Street. As a precaution, William Newby Colam, with his experience of the Highgate Hill, Edinburgh, Birmingham and Brixton cable tramways, was appointed as Design Engineer.

Dick, Kerr and Company won the contract to build the tramway. Owing to the narrow streets the line would be 3 ft 6 in gauge and mainly single track with passing loops at the termini and about three-quarters of a mile up the route at the junction with Smedley Street. The design of the passing loops was interesting. The Smedley Street and Crown Square loops meant that the normal rule of the road, driving on the left, applied. So each point had a straight path for the tramcar approaching into the facing direction while the car travelling in the trailing direction passed over the curved section, as this arrangement reduced the risk of derailment.

The passing loop at Smedley Street being laid. The configuration of the points means that the tramcar approaching the points will always take the straight path and leave the loop by the curved path. Watching the workmen seems a popular occupation.

The tramcar depot and winding house recently finished and waiting for the tramcars and the opening of the tramway.

The tramway Company claimed that the line was the steepest cable street tramway in the world with a rise of 1 in 5½. Laying the track started in 1891 with a 2 ft 9 in deep trench being dug and short yokes laid. Concrete was poured to form the conduit (which also acted as its own drain) and foundations for the running rails. The running rails were fixed on the foundation and secured with tie bars from the yokes. The slot rails were fixed giving a gap 11/16 inch wide. Hatches were fitted enabling access to pulleys, while the return pulleys at Crown Square were housed in a brick-lined room that the Engineers could enter through a manhole for inspection, maintenance and repairs.

The single line created a unique problem for the line. It had to ensure that the up and the down cables could operate in the same conduit just a few inches wide. On straight track it was simple to place two vertical pulleys next to each other to support the cables. However, the Matlock line had some sharp curves. This meant that the pulleys had to be designed to enable both cables to be guided around the curve while travelling in opposite directions and without interfering with the grip of tramcars using either cable. It seems that pulleys with only one large flange were used, rather than the more common 'V' section. The road surface was completed by laying setts made from Derbyshire Peak gritstone, giving a durable surface that gave grip to horses hauling other road traffic.

The cable was 3 in in circumference and was driven at a constant speed of 5½ mph and weighed four tons five hundredweight. The winding house and depot were built by W. Knowles and Son on land at the top of the tramway. It held two boilers that could generate steam at 100 lbs per square inch. The chimney became a notable feature of the town, being 100 ft tall. There were two steam engines, one of which provided the power with the other as a spare. The building also had an engineering shop for repairs and a waiting room with a ladies' cloak-room.

Three tramcars were purchased from G. F. Milnes and Company and, all to the same design. They were double-deck, open-top, short-canopy bogie tramcars with reversible garden seats on both decks. Each tramcar was fitted with two braking systems. The handbrake was used in normal operation, and acted on all eight wheels. There was also an emergency slot brake (located under the stairs). Both the brakes could be operated from either end of the car so, if required, the conductor could use either brake to stop the tramcar should the driver be unable to do so. Each tramcar carried two grips, one at each end and were of the side-entry type. The driver would operate the leading end grip, grasping the cable between two jaws, hauling the uphill car and acting as a brake on the downhill car. The only times the grip should have been relaxed was at the termini, the Smedley Street loop and the official stopping places. The tramcar would be drawn to a halt and held stationary by the handbrake.

The line was officially inspected by Major General Hutchinson on 1st March 1893. He agreed to the opening of the line subject to some easily implemented procedures. For example, when travelling up or down the hill, the conductor was required to stand on the rear platform, ready to operate the brakes should it become necessary. Also the gripper operating wheel should be removed from the trailing end of the car and a cap fitted over the top of the gripper shaft to prevent unauthorised persons interfering with it. He also required that a compulsory stop be required at the Smedley Street passing loop and that the upper terminus should be on the more level track at the entrance to the depot and not on the steep road. The written authorisation was issued on 15th March.

An opening ceremony was organised for 28th March with George Newnes as guest of honour. No less than five Committees were set up to look after arrangements for the day (one Committee had 29 members). The official party travelled by a large number of carriages from the railway station

Tramcar number 1 approaching the upper terminus with another tramcar parked just outside the depot.

to Crown Square. Here the party halted and the main guests stood on a stage. Newnes was presented with an album of photographs of the tramway, amid speeches. The party then ascended the hill to the depot. A large crowd of people lined the whole route to see the first tramcar descend from the depot to Crown Square at 2.37pm, Mrs Newnes having started the engines at 2.30pm. The party then moved to the Assembly Rooms for a banquet, at which 120 people were present. There were more speeches, toasts (all 14 of them) and a band played to the public at the depot and in Crown Square. The meal consisted of five courses. The public service commenced following the arrival of the first car and cars travelled full as people wanted to travel on the first day of operation. The Company was able to announce a dividend of 2% after nine months of operation.

Unfortunately, this did not continue. The economy of the country took a downturn, fewer folk were taking holidays and visitor numbers dropped. In 1895 the tramway made a loss, mainly due to the expenditure on a new cable. A fare rise was implemented, from a 1d each way to 2d up and 1d down.

Two tramcars wait at the lower terminus in Crown Square while an engineer works on one of the pulleys, with his arm down the access hatch. In fact this is a posed photograph, though the purpose behind it is unknown.

It would seem that the rules were not always adhered to. One story tells of drivers giving white knuckle rides to their passengers by releasing the tramcar from the cable when going downhill. The tram would accelerate under gravity and exceed the 5½ mph speed limit imposed on them. If passengers commented on the excessive speed the driver would tell them not to worry as the river would stop them if needed. Also, although conductors were instructed to remain on the rear platform in order to operate the brakes in an emergency, it was commented that children would sometimes jump on the rear step for a free ride, while the conductor was collecting fares from the upper deck.

For most of its life the tramway would operate with two tramcars, using the downward moving car to counterbalance the uphill car, in the same way as a funicular. However, this would not have worked for the whole line as the passing place was not at the halfway point. For about half the length of the journey from Crown Square to the loop at Smedley Street the downhill car would not be able to act as a counterbalance. The procedure was to start the uphill car first and to indicate to the driver of the downhill car when to leave, the aim being that they meet at the Smedley Street loop. On bank holidays all three cars would be put into service.

Initially there was one intermediate stop at Smedley Street. Passengers then got into the habit of asking the car to stop at various points on the journey. When these started to have an adverse effect on the timetable they were replaced with official stopping places at the Wesleyan Chapel and Smedley Street. A request from staff and visitors to Smedley's Memorial Hospital to also have a stop was initially rejected, but after a petition the stop was added to the official stopping places.

MATLOCK URBAN DISTRICT COUNCIL 1898 - 1927

From 1895 the tramway operation was discouraging, with receipts often lower than expenses. Indeed, in the winter of 1896 the condition of the cable deteriorated and the directors decided to halt the service until a new cable was fitted. Despite the fact that they had previously ordered one and it was waiting to be delivered, the tramway stayed closed until March when the new cable was delivered and finally fitted. No doubt the Directors would have liked to shut the tramway during the winter of 1897. However, matters were taken out of their hands. George Newnes (he had become Sir George in 1895) decided to withdraw from the Board of the tramway. He purchased all the shares and then, as the outright owner, gifted the tramway to the Matlock Urban District Council. The transfer of ownership took place on 24th June 1898. Typically for the period, a celebration was held, though, owing to commitments of Sir George, it did not take place until 20th October. The event was commemorated in a similar way as the opening, there was a banquet followed by a concert. Sir George was given a gold lifetime pass for travel on the tramway.

The Council held town celebrations to recognise the gift of the tramway to the Council. Clearly a great excuse for a party, the tramcar is almost completely hidden by the crowds.

Almost immediately the Council decided to apply for permission to extend the tramway to Matlock Bridge Station. Other extensions were added to the application and an Act was passed giving the necessary authority. While loans were being sought, reality appears to have overtaken optimism as Councillors started referring to the tramway as a "white elephant". All idea of expansion was dropped at the end of 1900 when the accounts showed a loss of nearly £500 during the previous eleven months. In 1903 a parcels service was introduced which generated up to six shillings per day. Parcels would be carried on the tram and then carried by porters to destinations up to half a mile from the tramway. For the next few years the tramway hovered around the break-even mark, sometimes showing a small profit and sometimes a small loss. The situation gradually got worse and from 1910 the line made a loss every year, a situation not helped by a series of cables that had to be renewed sooner than expected.

In 1911, the Council introduced a three car service which improved income, putting the tramway into a profit. They decided to purchase another tramcar and at this time the Birmingham cable tramway was being converted to electric operation and was disposing of their fleet. Matlock was going to buy two open-top bogie cars, but reduced this to one. The workshop at the depot took the tramcar and converted it to single-deck. The Council said that it was to be used to support the three car service. However, they clearly had a saving on running costs as a priority. Quite possibly the Council had in mind using the smaller and lighter car for the winter service. The three car service lasted for four years until the start of the First World War. This affected public transport around the country. As the war continued, large numbers of men were being sent to The Front and the number of holidaymakers declined. The Council decided to reduce the service from three cars to two, so the extra tramcar was no longer needed. Its demise may also have been prompted by the poor reception from the public. It had longitudinal seating which meant on the steep hill passengers slid down, ending up crowded against the lower bulkhead. Number 4 was withdrawn and sold. To add to the woes, replacement parts were both difficult and expensive to obtain. After the cessation of hostilities, the cost of labour rose and the Council found that the tramway deficit grew each year. In 1919 one of the boilers needed replacing. Rather than purchase a new steam boiler it was decided to change the technology and install a suction gas plant extracting gas to fuel a gas engine. Opening in 1921, they soon found that this was significantly less expensive than the previous system. Another issue arose in 1919 as the track was wearing out and needed repairing. The consequence was that, in the same year, the Council introduced a rise in the fares to 3d for the uphill journey and 1½d downhill with a 25% drop in patronage. This was followed in 1920 with another rise to 4d for the uphill journey and 2d downhill.

Things started to get better. In the latter half of 1920 the railways re-introduced excursion trains to Matlock (stopped during the war). The result was that from 1922 the tramway losses were greatly reduced. In 1924 the Council surprisingly reduced the fares to 2d for the uphill journey and 1d downhill. This lasted four months, before the Council increased the fares for the uphill journey to 3d for visitors and 1½d for ratepayers. However, the improvement was short-lived and by 1924 the tramway was incurring a worrying loss.

Having been given the tramway, the Council soon changed the owner's name on each tramcar by announcing "Matlock Urban District Council Tramway" along the frame over the side windows.

The passing loop at Smedley Road with tramcars 2 and 3.

This began a long debate on its future. Various ideas were put forward from time to time, mainly to replace the tramway with a bus service. However, all such proposals failed to get sufficient votes to be accepted. Then on 20th June 1926 a vote was passed to reduce the tramway Manager's pay. The Chairman of the Tramways Committee objected and resigned from the Committee. The anti-tramway Councillors were in the majority and the end of the tramway was looming. The residents of the town were split, but there were not enough supporting the pro-tramway camp to change the Council's mind. The Council negotiated with local bus operators for them to operate joint services to replace the tramway. Negotiations were a little fraught, with arguments between the different bus Companies. As negotiations began to reach agreement the tramway itself helped the Council make up its mind. A strand on the cable broke on 23rd September 1927. It was decided it would cost too much to effect repairs and a temporary bus service was started. The newly agreed permanent bus service began on 1st October. The tramway ended with a whimper rather than a bang.

Tramcar number 2 at the Crown Square terminus. The official at the back of the tram with the wheel barrow is working on the parcels service. He will have placed his load of parcels onto the driver's platform, who will keep them secure during the journey up the hill.

THE CABLE TRAMWAY FLEET

MATLOCK TRAMWAY COMPANY LIMITED 1893 - 1898

Fleet number	Date built	Builder	Type	Number of seats
1 - 3	1893	G. F. Milnes & Co.	Open top, bogie	13/18

Livery
The livery was royal blue and white with gold lining. The company's name appeared on a monogram crest on the sides of the car.

A poor photograph, taken from the High Peak News, 28th March 1914. It is included as it is the only photograph found that shows the single deck car number 4.

MATLOCK URBAN DISTRICT COUNCIL TRAMWAY 1898 - 1927

Fleet number	Date built	Builder	Type	Number of seats
1 - 3	1893	G. F. Milnes & Co.	Open – top, bogie	13/18
4	1911	Matlock Tramway	Single- deck, bogie†	?

Notes

† Number 4 was purchased second-hand from Birmingham Tramways Company in 1911. It was originally built as an open top bogie tramcar in 1898 by Metropolitan Railway Carriage and Wagon Company Limited. The Matlock Tramway rebuilt it to single deck and it enabled a three car service to be run until that was abandoned in 1914. Then, surplus to requirements, it was withdrawn and sold. One of its less enamouring features was longitudinal seating. Whilst frequently used on lower saloon seating of tramcars, it did mean that on the steep Matlock hill the passengers all slid down, becoming close friends, whether or not they wanted to.

Livery

The livery was royal blue and white with gold lining. The Council's name appeared on the Council crest on the sides of the car. The cars were later renamed with an identification "Matlock Urban District Council Tramway" on the frame above the windows.

REFERENCES

The Matlock Steep-gradient Tramway, 1893, reprinted 1972 by The Arkwright Society
The Matlock Cable Tramway, by C. C. Hall, Tramway Review, 1951
Tuppence Up, Penny Down, by M. J. Arkle, published by the author
North Derbyshire Tramways, by Barry M. Marsden 2002; Tempus Publishing Ltd.
Nottingham and Derbyshire Tramway, by Barry M. Marsden, 2005, Middleton Press
The Matlock Cable Tramway, by Glynn Waite, 2012, Pynot Publishing

The River Derwent occasionally flooded, affecting Crown Square. The cable tramcars are one of the few forms of street transport that can continue to operate in quite deep water. The cable continues to run, though no passengers want to alight into the water.

CHAPTER 8

ISLE OF MAN

UPPER DOUGLAS CABLE TRAMWAY 1896 - 1929

ISLE OF MAN TRAMWAY AND ELECTRIC POWER COMPANY 1896 - 1902

The Douglas and Laxey Coast Electric Tramway Company (D&LCET) were the owners of the Manx Electric Railway (MER) and the Snaefell Mountain Railway. The start of the MER was situated at the far northern end of the bay from the Douglas landing pier. Running along the whole of the promenade, and linking the two, was the Douglas Bay horse tramway. It was an essential link to bring prospective passengers to the MER and so the D&LCET approached the horse tramway with the aim of purchasing it, as they wished to be in control. The sale took place in May 1894 and the Company changed its name to the Isle of Man Tramway and Electric Power Company (IoMT&EP). At this time there were just three years left on the lease of the tramway. The Company wanted to electrify the horse line and link it directly to the MER, which would enable MER trams to run along the promenade to the landing pier. The local horse cab drivers resisted and used their connections with hotel and shop owners along the promenade to oppose the development. At the same time the Company was seeking an extension of the lease to operate the horse tramway. However, the Company was not alone and a second bid was made for the horse tramway lease. At this time, the Douglas Town Commissioners were receiving representations from residents of the upper town to build a tramway, as two attempts at running horse buses had failed due to the steepness of the hills. Many upper town residents had been refusing to pay their rates in protest. The IoMT&EP decided to take the initiative and offered to build the tramway to the upper town and to supply free electricity to light the promenade in exchange for a 21-year lease on the horse tramway and authorisation to double the track and to convert it to electrical operation. While the horse tramway was built along the level promenade, ideal for horse operation, the upper town was built on a steep hill and a different form of power would be needed. Indeed, no form of propulsion relying on adhesion of the wheels on the rails was suitable. The recently opened cable tramways in Edinburgh were visited and it was concluded that cable was the solution to the problem of the hill.

Looking very smartly turned out, tramcar number 82 pauses on the single track near the depot.

Track being laid along Prospect Hill. Note the sequence starts with the yokes and slot rails, forming the cable conduit. being laid before the running rails.

After further negotiations, the Company and Douglas Commissioners agreed to jointly promote a Bill in Tynwald and to build the cable tramway as quickly as possible. The Bill had a second reading and became an Act on 8th November 1895. The Act defined the route length as 1⅜ miles going from The Peveril Hotel near the landing pier, along Victoria Street, Prospect Hill, Bucks Road, Ballaquayle Road and Broadway to terminate at the promenade. Most of the 3 ft gauge tramway was to be double track, using interlaced track sections at sharp curves. The Act defined the charges for fares and carrying luggage and parcels.

Dick, Kerr and Company were contracted to build the tramway, the choice possibly being influenced by knowing that the Company had experience building the Brixton Hill, Matlock and two routes in Edinburgh. Construction began in January 1896, including a short piece of demonstration double track to show (using horse trams) the clearances available for other road traffic. Once shop owners along Victoria Street and Prospect Hill saw the line of the tracks, they petitioned the Company to put the double track along the centre of the road, rather than as two single lines along the sides of the road. The local newspaper warned that this contravened the detail in the Act. Work on that section of the line was halted and, since the authorities wanted the tramway as quickly as possible, an amendment to the Act was rushed through. Construction continued, though it was hindered a little by some of the other services buried in the road, the main culprits being water and gas pipes that seemed to occupy the line of the tramway conduit, so a degree of pipe relaying was necessary. Each 3 ft gauge track (the same gauge as the horse tramway and the MER) consisted of the two running rails and the central conduit with its longitudinal slot. The yokes for the conduit and its slot were short, supporting only the slot rails and connected to the running rails by tie bars. The yokes were set every 3 ft 6 in. The slot was 11/16 in wide (1/16 in wider on curves) and the conduit tube was 19 in deep by 9 in wide, made by pouring concrete around formers. Every 49 ft along the track were pulley pits incorporating drainage and vertical 12 in diameter pulleys to support the cable. At curves horizontal pulleys, 12 in in diameter, were fitted at much closer intervals to guide the cable around the arcs.

The 3½ in circumference cable was delivered in one length in July 1896. However, it weighed 20 tons and, as the crane at Douglas harbour could only lift 15 tons, the cable, made by George Craddock, Wakefield, had to be wound on two reels. Getting it up to the winding house was fraught. Two traction engines were used to haul the cable up the hill, but they could not get enough grip and halted short of the journey. They only succeeded when assisted by ropes and winches. The two traction engines were used again in August 1896 to feed the cable into the conduit. Starting at the winding house they pulled the cable through the conduit, around most of the tramway route. They were prevented from completing the route because of road works. So a rope was laid across the obstacle and the cable pulled through. The traction engines pulled the cable back to the winding house. The whole business had taken 29 hours. The final task was to splice the ends of the cable together to become endless (the splice was 80 ft long). The operation was completed on 7th August 1896. One engine was started and the cable was operated. When the engineers were satisfied that all was well, a tramcar was sent out on a test run. A second cable, made by T. and W. Smith, Newcastle, was delivered and stored in the winding house (cables were expected to be replaced every fifteen months).

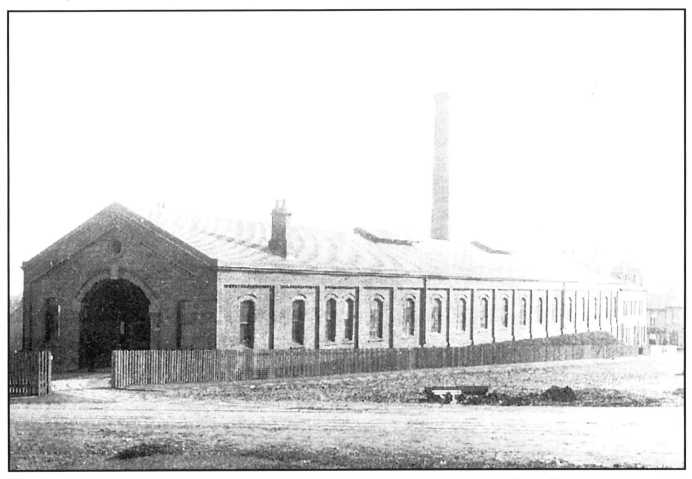

The tramcar depot and winding house (behind the depot) at York Road.

In the winding house the boilers and engines were duplicated, ensuring there was always a spare. Only one engine was needed to drive the tramway, the other was a spare for use during maintenance or the breakdown of the other. The engines were supplied by Dick, Kerr and Company and each was rated at 250 hp. The grip pulley was 10 ft in diameter and the cable was held for almost 75% of its circumference by an idler pulley. A third pulley was held on a carriage that was pulled back by a tension weight to keep the cable taut. The engines drove the cable on the track furthest from the building. This was to ensure that the tramcars could run freely on the downhill track when the grip was released and lifted from the cable to clear the diverter pulleys. Alongside the winding house was the depot building housing the fleet. It could accommodate 21 cars.

The interior of the tramcar depot prior to the opening of the system. Two of the tramcars have been delivered and are stored in the shed.

For the opening of the line, twelve tramcars were ordered from G. F. Milnes & Co., although only four were delivered in time for the commencement of services, making early photographs of the interior of the depot seem very empty. The fleet numbers of the tramcars started at 71, to differentiate them from the horse trams and the MER fleet. Eight of the initial fleet were single-deck bogie crossbench cars with open sides, while four were single-deck bogie saloon cars, particularly for winter use. Every tramcar had a driving position and grip at each end, one for each direction of travel. Tramcars could enter the depot from either direction, but at the building entrance there was a single track. This led to a traverser allowing the tramcar to be moved sideways to move onto any of the four tracks. The cable went to the engines that were in the building to the side of the depot, so the storage area was cable free. It did mean that moving the tramcars in the depot meant man-power, so staff pushed cars along. The arrangement was slightly different at the entrance. Two curves joined at the entrance, one from the north, uphill of the depot, and one from the south, downhill of the depot. A tramcar heading for the depot would enter from the higher entrance curve using gravity to take it onto the traverser. When leaving the depot a tramcar would be given a gentle push to start it rolling down the other curve and gravity would take it far enough for the car to take up the cable.

A cable tramcar from the 79 - 82 series waits at the Victoria Street terminus while a horse tram makes its way along the promenade towards Derby Castle.

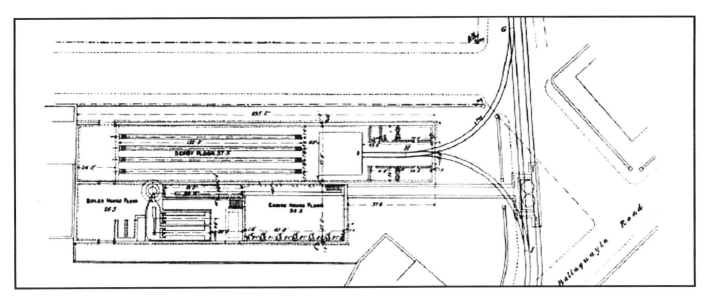

The tramcar depot and winding house at York Road.

In the depot each storage siding had a maintenance pit along most of its length. Steps at each end of the pit allowed staff to descend into the pit and to get access beneath the tramcar. There was sufficient room to store 21 tramcars, although the maximum number the line ever had was 16. Each tramcar had two grips, these were made to the design previously patented by William Colam (who had been Assistant to cable tramway pioneer William Eppelsheimer on the Highgate Hill line).

There were two separate braking systems. A wheel brake operated by acting on all eight wheels of the tramcar. For most of the time the speed of the tramcars would be limited by the speed of the cable. This was originally set in the Act as 8 mph, however, the authorities felt this was too fast for the section from Hill Street to Thomas Street where a local 6 mph speed limit was fixed.

The terminus at Victoria Street, where the cable tramway met the horse tram.

Number 73 waits in Ballaquayle Road. The absence of building further up the hill shows that this photograph was taken early in the life of the tramway.

Since there was just the one cable, this ruling meant that the whole of the system was limited to 6 mph. The wheel brakes were mainly used at the terminals, to hold the tramcar in place, or at those places where the tramcar released the cable at stops and where the cable diverted to the winding house. To assist the efficiency of the wheel brakes, sand boxes were fitted to the tramcars allowing the driver to drop sand in front of the wheels and increase the friction between the wheel tread and rail. There was a second brake system, the emergency brake, acting on the slot rails. The slot brake had been designed by the Dick, Kerr Engineer, James More, based on the one used at Matlock. It passed through the slot with blocks above and below the slot rails that could be clamped together bringing the tramcar to a sudden halt. It was also removable when the tramcar was moved into the depot.

James Walker, the Engineer of the island's Harbour Board, was invited to formally inspect the line. On 8th August 1896 he travelled over the line to examine the standard of construction. The first problem he encountered was at Avondale House where the slot brake fouled the slot. He also specified that there should be a test of the slot brake on the steepest part of the line on Prospect Hill, and finally he instructed that warning bells had to be fitted under the roof canopies at each end of the cars. Three local men had been recruited as drivers and they spent three weeks in Edinburgh training. On return, they, and some drivers from Edinburgh and London, arrived on the island to train more staff.

Mr Walker's assistant was able to report on 13th August that the changes specified during the inspection had been met and the tramway could open. It opened to the public on 15th August with the four tramcars that had been delivered. As additional trams were delivered they entered service. The formal opening was on 26th August 1896, when a procession of dignitaries travelled by cable car from Broadway through Upper Douglas and down to the promenade, changing onto a horse tram for the remainder of the journey to Derby Castle. Then they returned by horse car to the Castle Hotel on the promenade where speeches were made praising the new tramway. In the evening of the following day there was a visit to the winding house and depot for invited guests, followed by a sumptuous dinner at the Douglas Bay Hotel, hosted by the tramway Company and Dick, Kerr and Company.

There were a few teething issues but, on the whole, the tramway performed well carrying over half a million passengers a year. After just over three years the whole island received a great shock. One of the island's major banks, Dumbells, ran out of money and had to shut in January 1900. The bank's General Manager was the same Alexander Bruce who was Chairman of the Isle of Man Tramway and Electric Power Company, owner of all the tramways on the island. What had not been appreciated was that the financial successes of the tramways were riding on loans from the bank. The generous dividends being paid to shareholders did not come from profits, but loans from Dumbell's Bank. The tramways continued to run while the future of the Company was being decided, whether to seek further loans to continue trading or to liquidate the Company. The decision was taken out of the shareholders' hands when a creditor petitioned the court to wind-up the Company. In June 1900 the court appointed a Receiver and when the Company could not demonstrate a plan to save the Company, declared it liquidated. The Receiver started making arrangements to sell the assets to recover as much money as possible for the creditors. Tenders were invited for the tramway undertakings.

DOUGLAS CORPORATION 1902 - 1929

Douglas Corporation was no doubt placed under pressure to take some measure to ensure public transport for the town. They also saw an opportunity of acquiring the tramways at a knock down price. In August 1901 the Corporation made a bid of £40,000 for the horse tramway and the cable tramway (the latter being described by the valuer as "a dead loss"). This was refused and a revised bid of £50,000 was made in September 1901 and was accepted. In the meantime, bids for the Snaefell and MER lines were all found unacceptable. The situation was finally resolved when the electric tramway Companies were sold in November 1902.

Tramcar number 77 was delivered in 1896 as a crossbench car. It was modified in 1903 by fitting side panels to form an enclosed saloon. Note the ownership of the tramway by the Corporation has been prominently recorded on the rocker panel. The photograph was taken at the Victoria Street terminus.

In 1901 the service of the cable tramway from the depot in York Road to the promenade via Ballaquayle Road had ceased, due to the silting-up of the terminus pulley pit at Broadway, though the cable continued to run under that section. An early decision under Corporation management was to shorten the cable by rebuilding the northern terminus at Stanley View. The reduced length of cable meant that there were appreciable savings on the coal consumption of the boilers. A new section of track was built from the new terminus, along Waverley Road to a new horse tram shed, built on ground beside the cable tram depot. This track did not join with the cable track and horse cars had to be manhandled off the cable track onto the new siding in order to store them. The, now abandoned, track between Stanley View and Broadway was lifted and recycled on the horse tramway. The cable tramway was given fixed stopping places, recognisable by having cast iron stops signs, previously intending passengers would hail the tramcar at any point. In the winter of 1902 crossbench car number 78 had its sides panelled in order to supplement the four saloon cars. This evidently was well received by the public as number 77 was similarly rebuilt in the winter of 1903, though to a less expensive specification.

With an eye on increasing customer numbers, the Corporation sought to extend the line from Victoria Street to Victoria Pier. The Harbour Commissioners refused the request and instead the Corporation had to use its horse trams to carry people arriving by ferry from the pier to the cable terminus.

In 1907 two new tramcars were purchased from The United Electric Car Company and entered service as numbers 69 and 70. A third tramcar, number 68, was purchased from G. C. Milnes, Voss and Company in 1909 and a fourth, number 67, in 1911.

Up until 1908 the tramway had run without any fatalities, however, that year there were two. A pedestrian with sight impairment walked in front of a tramcar and was fatally injured. The second death was of an employee, a stoker in the boiler house, who had died of heat stroke on a hot summer's day.

In 1907 the Corporation purchased two new tramcars from the United Electric Car Company in Preston. These were numbered 69 and 70, being given numbers that preceded the existing cable car fleet. Intended to attract passengers on summer days, they were also fitted with wooden roller blinds for less clement weather.

There had been no Sunday service, but this changed in 1911 when the town saw trams running on the Sabbath. During the First World War the tramways continued to run, though with a reduced service. The standard of maintenance deteriorated with the shortage of replacement parts and by the end of the hostilities the line required substantial renovation. In 1922, the Corporation purchased Tilling petrol-electric buses and these took over the tramway route during the winter (a time when the tramway always lost money). The Corporation was loath to spend money on a service that at best broke even, but usually lost money. In 1929 the effect of the British depression meant that few could afford holidays and visitor numbers plummeted. The decision was taken that this was to be the final season and, when the buses took over for the winter, the cable tramway would close for good. The last tramcars ran on 19th August 1929.

The first job undertaken was to remove the cable and fill in the conduit. The track was lifted later. The depot became a bus garage while the boilers and engines were broken up in the winding house. The sixteen tramcars were sold with the purchaser having the idea to convert them into holiday cottages. Only two were actually sold and the remainder were scrapped. In 1968 these two, numbers 72 and 73, were moved to the old depot and restored into a single car carrying both numbers. The restored car was paraded along the horse tramway on special occasions, including taking part in the horse tramway centenary procession in August 1976. At first it had to be towed by a Land Rover, later it was powered using an electric motor energised by batteries. In 2010 it was moved to the Jurby Transport Museum, where it continues to be an exhibit.

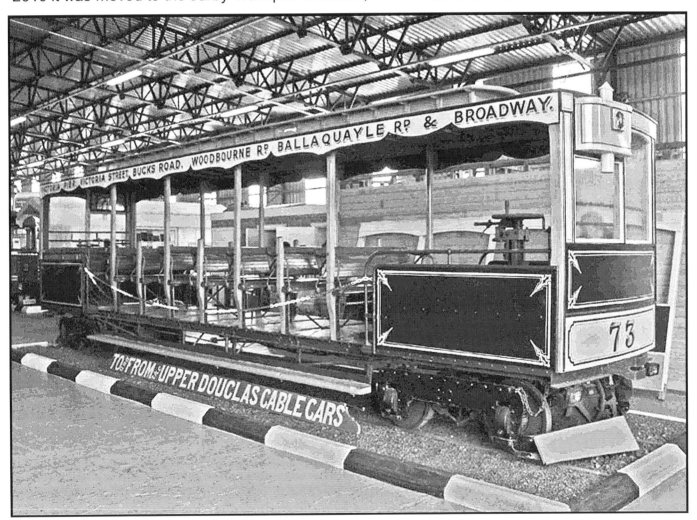

The restored cable tramcar numbers 72 and 73 (each dash panel carries a different number) is exhibited in the Jurby Transport Museum. Since restoration it has run on the horse tramway towed by a Land Rover, later under its own power having been equipped with electric motors and batteries. In the museum it is a static exhibit.

TRAMWAY FLEET

ISLE OF MAN TRAMWAY AND ELECTRIC POWER COMPANY 1896 - 1902

Fleet number	Date built	Builder	Type	Number of seats
71 – 78	1896	G. F. Milnes & Co.	Crossbench	38
79 - 82	1896	G. F. Milnes & Co.	Saloon	32

Livery
Blue and white.

Above: Number 77 in its initial form. After the Corporation took over the operation of the tramway they rebuilt this car and number 78 with central saloons.

Below: From the first batch of tramcars is number 72, parts of the car were used in the restoration of preserved car number 72/73

TRAMWAY FLEET

DOUGLAS CORPORATION 1902 - 1929

Fleet number	Date built	Builder	Type	Number of seats
67	1911	G. C. Milnes, Voss & Co.	Crossbench†	38
68	1909	G. C. Milnes, Voss & Co.	Crossbench‡	38
69, 70	1907	United Electric Car Co.	Crossbench‡	38
71 – 76	1896	G. F. Milnes & Co.	Crossbench	38
77	1896	G. F. Milnes & Co.	Crossbench^	38
78	1896	G. F. Milnes & Co.	Crossbench^^	38
79 - 82	1896	G. F. Milnes & Co.	Saloon	32

Notes

† Fitted with side canvas screens for the protection of passengers
‡ Fitted with side wooden roller blinds for the protection of passengers
^ Converted to combination car in 1903
^^ Converted to combination car in 1902

Livery
Blue and white.

REFERENCES

The Douglas Cable Tramway Engine Room, The Engineer, 23rd October 1896
Isle of Man Tramways, by F. K. Pearson, 1970, David & Charles
Cable Tram Days, by F. K. Pearson, 1977, Douglas Cable Car Group
Double Century, by Stan Basnett & Keith Pearson, 1996, Adam Gordon

Tramcar number 78 in its rebuilt form. Originally a crossbench car constructed by G. C. Milnes and Company in 1896, it was given a saloon in 1902.

CHAPTER 9

SWANSEA

SWANSEA CONSTITUTION HILL INCLINE TRAMWAY 1898 - 1901

It has been said that Constitutional Hill in Swansea is the steepest road in the British Isles. These days it presents a very stiff climb for the pedestrian, though not for wheeled traffic as it is now a one-way street for descending vehicles only. It was used as part of a challenging stage for the 2010 cycling Tour of Britain competition. However, for this occasion, the cyclists were required to take the uphill route.

Back in Victorian days the town of Swansea (it was granted city status in 1969) was expanding and a new workhouse was built in 1862 on Mount Pleasant (in an area unfortunately named "Gibbethill"). The area close by, called "Townhill", was recognised by the Council as being suitable for housing development because it was above the smoke of the many copper furnaces in the town and it had splendid views over the bay. The Council and the Garden Suburb Freehold Company Limited (owned by the Duke of Beaufort) were both part-owners of the land. However, the developers involved in building the houses were concerned that prospective purchasers might be deterred by the stiff climb up the hill. The development started in the early 1890s and a group of local entrepreneurs sought a way of overcoming the deterrent of the steep hill. The chosen route was the most direct to Townhill, up Constitution Hill, a road that had an average gradient of 1 in 5 with parts at 1 in 3.5. The chosen solution was that of a cable tramway and the managing director of a fuel Company, William Bondfield Westlake, volunteered to fund its building. The Swansea Constitution Hill Incline Tramway Company Limited was established on 26th April 1897 with the intention of buying the tramway when it had been built. William Westlake agreed with the Company that he would pay for the construction and the Company would purchase it for £8,212 and operate it when it was ready to carry passengers.

SWANSEA CONSTITUTION HILL INCLINE TRAMWAY.

—

THIS TRAMWAY WILL BE

OPEN FOR THE PUBLIC

TO-MORROW (SATURDAY) MORNING,

AUGUST 27th, 1898, AT 9 A.M.

—

FARE — — — — ONE PENNY.

Announcement in the local newspapers for the opening of the Constitution Hill cable tramway.

An application was made in 1896 for an Order authorising the building of the tramway to take passengers between the lower terminus at Hannover Street (then named St George Street) and the upper terminus at Terrace Road. Authority was granted for the building of a funicular-type cable tramway. The line was to be 925 feet long with a climb of 185 feet. The Order stated that the track should be interlaced with a 130 ft long passing loop halfway up. It was actually built as a single track with points enabling the tramcars to pass at the loop, which caused problems a little later (the lower half of the tramway may have been interlaced). The gauge of the track was 3 ft 6 in and the road surface was made up with granite cobblestones.

The company hired George Croydon Marks as the Consulting Engineer, who had experience of building funiculars at Lynton and Lynmouth (opened 1890), Bridgnorth (opened 1892) and the cable tramway at Matlock (opened 1893). Both funiculars were powered using water tanks under the cars to ensure that the upper carriage was heavier than the lower carriage, using gravity to move the cars up and down the track. The Matlock tramway used the continuously moving endless cable system. Clearly, the water counterbalance system was not suitable for a street tramway and the system would have to be powered using an engine driving the cable. There appeared to be no plans to have a link with the existing horse tramway. Clearly the mode of propulsion was entirely different and the gauge was not the same (the horse tramway was standard gauge).

A view of the whole tramway, with one car at the upper terminal and the other at the bottom. As it was a funicular the tramcars stayed out in the road all the time. The winding house was near the top of the tramway.

George Webb and Company of Westminster were contracted by the Company to build the line. It was constructed with an underground conduit between the rails of the track to take the 3½ in circumference cable. The conduit had a slot along its length that allowed a metal plate to be fixed under the tramcar that went through the slot and was attached to an end of the cable. The cable was guided through the conduits by pulleys set at around 50 ft apart, those along the part of the road where it became steeper were mounted above the cable to prevent it from lifting out of the slot. Unlike the continuous type of cable tramway, the cable at Swansea went from one tramcar, up the hill to the return pulley and then back down to the other tramcar. There was no cable downhill of each tramcar and the return pulley was also the driving pulley. The diameter of the return pulley was significantly larger than the distance apart of the running cables. Two smaller pulleys, one each side of the cables, were fitted that pushed the cables to the correct position to run in the joint conduit of the upper single line section. Whilst on the continuous cable tramway the cable ran constantly, the funicular only operated the cable when the two cars were due to move. Also the cars were permanently attached to the ends of the cable. The two major factors causing wear to the cable were eliminated, because for the majority of the time the cable was stationary, and there was no heavy load caused by friction when the tramcar grips clamped to the cable. The main disadvantage to using the funicular system in a street is at the passing place. The standard rule for British roads is to drive on the left, allowing oncoming traffic to pass on your right. On a funicular this practice can only operate in this way at the passing loop for half of its journeys. Each car must always take the same side of the loop each time they pass, whether going up or down, and so breaks the rule of the road 50% of the time. On Constitution Hill the steep hill meant that it was extremely unlikely that there would be any other traffic apart from a few pedestrians.

The winding house was located at the top of the tramway. As the tramcars spent the nights out in the road there was no tramcar depot.

The winding house was built at the top of the hill on the corner of Constitution Hill and Terrace Road, on the right hand side when looking up the hill. It was equipped with two Tangye gas engines, one being the reserve during the operation of the other. For reasons unknown the two engines were different sizes; one was rated at 16 hp while the other had almost 25% less power at 13 hp. Each was connected via its own clutch (supplied by D. Bridge and Company of Salford) to a shaft running underground to the return pulley at the top of the track. The engine driver in the confines of the winding house was unable to see the tramcars or the state of the road. To assist him there were two aids. One of the top guidance pulleys was connected to a dial showing the position of the tramcars on the track, thus enabling him to slow and stop them at the appropriate places. It is not recorded if there were any intermediate stops on the route. This is possible as the Lynton and Lynmouth funicular was built with a request stop (removed many years ago) part the way down the track. In that instance the drivers of the cars actually rode on them and controlled them by using the brakes. There was a second communication through an overhead wire. No doubt many passengers thought that the tramcars had their own electric motors that provided the power. In fact, the overhead wire was a simple form of telegraph communication.

Overhead standards and cables were erected along the street and double wires (one for each tramcar) were carried for the full length of the line with an offset trolley pole mounted on each tramcar. Each tramcar carried its own dry batteries to power the telegraph. Operationally when the car at the lower terminus was ready to depart, the conductor would activate the telegraph and a bell would ring at the winding house and the upper tramcar. The engine driver would then start the engine and move the tramcars. It is possible that passengers could request the tramcars to stop to allow them off at any point on the hill, though, given the minimal length of the line, such stops would probably have been rare.

As previously mentioned, the system had two carriages, one fixed at each end of the cable. They were built by the Brush Electrical Engineering Company Limited and each had four wheels. There was seating for eighteen people on reversible seats and, in view of the steepness of the of the hill, the seats were set at an angle to make sitting down more comfortable. Since there were only two tramcars, there was no need to number them (very typical of funiculars). Each tramcar weighed around three tons and the tramcars had lever-operated wheel brakes, which would have been used to hold the tramcars at the termini when the number of passengers on each would change. However, given that the line was very short and that a standard fare of 1d was charged for journeys up or down, the take-up for downward journeys would have been low. Normal operation would have seen the upward bound tramcar having far more passengers than the downward bound tramcar. There was a second braking system on each car with two slot brakes. These were emergency brakes that clamped onto the metal sides of the slot, bringing the tramcar to a sudden halt.

In April 1898 the line was completed and the Board of Trade Inspector, Lt-Col. H. A. Yorke, visited the town to inspect it. His report was not what the promoters wanted. He refused to allow the line to open on the grounds that it was in too dangerous a condition to allow the public to ride on it. The first in a long list of shortcomings came when a test was carried out where the top tramcar was left empty while the bottom tramcar was fully loaded. When the engine was started the wire cable just slipped on the driving pulley, leaving the tramcars stationary. This led to the conclusion that if the loading were the other way around the engine driver would have no control over the tramcars. The weight difference would cause the wire to slip and the tramcars to run away. The tramcar driver would then be reliant on the wheel brakes, which a previous demonstration had been found wanting if the tramcars ran away. This was considered too dangerous, as was the arrangement at the passing loop. The Inspector criticised the large gap that existed where the two slots merged at the loop, which he considered too dangerous. These items, with other short-falls, required attention before authority could be given to open the line to the public.

The Company did its best to minimise a loss of confidence in its scheme and managed to keep the news out of the newspapers and magazines. It also had the task of working to correct the criticisms and satisfy the BoT Inspector. No doubt feeling aggrieved, the Company referred to the contract and refused to pay William Westlake the balance of the cost of the tramway, as it had failed the BoT inspection and was not able to be opened. Westlake, naturally, blamed the contractor, George Webb and Company. A new board was appointed (they were the four largest shareholders, all local businessmen). A local solicitor was appointed as Company Secretary

The passing loop halfway up the line. The overhead wire and trolley poles were part of the communications system, though may have fooled some passengers into thinking they were electric trams.

and the registered offices moved to Swansea. It was claimed that the Company could organise the necessary rectification work by using the money owing to William Westlake and this is what they proceeded to do. Around this time, technical magazines were publishing patents modifying driving pulleys to give greater grip on the cable. Details are scarce but it would seem that the Company was able to satisfy the Inspector as, when Major Sir Francis Marindin arrived on 7th August 1898 from the BoT, he inspected and ran tests on the line. One test was to load one tram-car with 2.5 tons of iron and the car was then allowed to run away. The crew used the emergency brake and stopped it within ten feet. The Inspector was satisfied and issued the certificate on 11th August 1898.

The tramway finally opened to the public at 9.00 am on 27th August 1898. The aim was to run a service from 11.00am to 11.15 pm every day except Sundays. Unfortunately, the tramway had a problem and had to be halted and it remained closed for another week. However, after that, it ran reliably carrying over 500 passengers each day over the 2½ minute journey. To try to increase business, the downhill fare was reduced to ½d. It was soon apparent that income did not meet expenditure. One reason was that the tramway required five men to staff it while it was running. It had two crew per tram (no doubt a BoT requirement; today the Great Orme Tramway only has one operator per tramcar, despite far stricter health and safety legislation) plus the engine driver.

The tramway continued to lose money, but was allowed to continue running. The likely explanation is that many of the shareholders had interests in the property developments at the top of the hill. By 1901 most of the developments had been completed and the tramway no longer served any purpose for the shareholders. They closed the tramway and the exact date is not known but is likely to be late 1901 or early 1902. In June 1903 the company tried to sell the tramway, but the only offer they had was £150 from the Swansea Council, which was swiftly rejected. The line was offered to a scrap merchant, but a local resident offered a higher bid and purchased it. It was offered to the Council for £140, but they placed the offer "on the table" and no decision was made. Towards the end of 1903 the track was taken up and the tramcars moved. The tramway Company was dissolved in 1905. John Price wrote an article about the tramway in the December 1979 issue of Modern Tramway whose title made his views quite clear "A Tramway Fiasco".

THE TRAMWAY FLEET

CONSTITUTION HILL CABLE TRAMWAY 1898 - 1901

Fleet number	Date built	Builder	Type	Number of seats
1 – 2†	1898	Brush Electrical Engineering Co. Ltd.	Single deck, 4 wheel	18

Note
† There is no indication whether the tramcars were numbered. The Act authorising the Great Orme tramway (another funicular) specified that those tramcars had to be numbered.

Livery
Not known.

REFERENCES

Swansea Constitution Hill Tramway, Tramway and Railway World, November 1899
A Tramway Fiasco, by J. H. Price, Modern Tramway December 1979
The Tramways of South Wales, by W. H. Bett & J. C. Gillham, edited by J. H. Price, 1993, Light Rail Transit Association

CHAPTER 10

LLANDUDNO

GREAT ORME CABLE TRAMWAY 1902—Date

GREAT ORME TRAMWAYS COMPANY 1902 – 1934

The Great Orme cable tramway is unusual in many respects. Possibly the main claim to fame is that it continues to operate and is the oldest, indeed the only, street cable tramway in the country. To be pedantic it is actually two tramways, each taking passengers half the distance to the summit with a change of tramcar and a short walk for users at the halfway station. The lower tramway is a funicular with the cable running in a conduit set between the running rails. The upper tramway is on a private right of way that is open to the public. There is no conduit, the cables run in the open between the rails. The town of Llandudno had two tramways. There was the Llandudno and Colwyn Bay Electric Railway Company Limited that opened in 1907 and operated until 1956 and the Great Orme Tramway (also at times called Railway). The operations never met, the closest they got was around one third of a mile. Similarly, there was never any business link.

The lower section of the tramway was completed first and the workers travelling to the half way station used trams 4 and 5 to take them to work on the upper section.

In the late 1800s Llandudno was developing as a holiday resort. The Great Orme forms a promontory north-west of the town with extensive views from the summit, looking over Anglesey, the north-west coast and the Isle of Man, as well as inland to the North Wales mountains. It was a popular place to visit, but with a stiff walk to get to the summit. Businessmen in the town suggested laying a tramway, though the steepness of the route meant a cable system would have to be used. A group of entrepreneurs got together to build the line. A Parliamentary Bill was obtained in 1898 authorising its building. It took two years for the group to raise sufficient capital to start construction. The contract to build the mechanics of the line was given to R. White & Son while a local company, Thomas and John Owen (John Owen was one of the promotors of the line), undertook the buildings. Construction started in April 1901. The line ran along Old Road, a street so narrow that it was necessary to close it while tram laying was completed. The timescale of the building was found to be too optimistic and building over-ran into the next year. The lower section was then complete and Colonal Von Donop was invited to carry out his inspection. He arrived on

30th July 1902 and approved the line. Since everything was running much later than planned, the Company opened the line for public service the next day, 31st July, without any opening ceremony. Construction of the upper section continued and Colonel Van Donop carried out his inspection on 8th May 1903 and required that the brakes on the tramcars needed modification. He was invited back on 7th July and gave his approval. The upper section was opened to the public the next day 8th July 1903.

The Act authorised the Company to build and open a hotel on the summit. However, the Company had used all its capital in building the tramway. The Company persuaded G. B. Morgan, owner of the Clarence Hotel in the town, to help fund the hotel and he became a director of the Company. He obtained backing from a local brewery allowing the Company to buy the Telegraph Inn at the summit. The Company started to rebuild and extend the original inn. To keep up income generation a marquee was put up that served beer and meals. Land was leased by Morgan to build a golf course at the summit. Unfortunately, he went bankrupt in 1904 and the Company was obliged to use some of its profits to complete construction of the buildings.

The lower tramway track, called the Great Orme Tramway, was built in the usual fashion for cable tramways. The gauge is 3 ft 6 in and, being in the roadway, it would have been expected that the rail would be tramway type grooved rail. However, the Board of Trade specified that the lower tramway should be made with ordinary flat bottom rail with a continuous check rail. The rails were bolted to longitudinal timber sleepers that were set in concrete. The conduit had deep 'Z' rails forming the slot, while the conduit was cast in concrete. Unusually for a cable tramway, there were no metal yokes in the construction of the track, the running rails being attached to the 'Z' rails with tie bars. From the lower terminus, Victoria Station, the line is single track along Old Road, which was widened to a minimum of 16ft. The slot on the conduit is1¼ in wide, while the conduit itself is 6 in wide and 14 in deep. At the top of Old Road the route turns left to run along the uphill side of Ty-Gwyn Road where the passing loop is located. This road had to be widened to a minimum of 23 ft, plus a 3 ft wide pavement. Above the loop, the track is interlaced all the way to the winding house, again running alongside the road. This section, although not in the road, is paved with the cable still in a conduit with access hatches for maintenance and repair of the pulleys. The pulleys are positioned to allow the cable to run freely while ensuring that it does not rub against the side of the narrow concrete conduit. The reason for the interlaced track is to keep the two cables separate, something not necessary on the section below the passing loop as this part of the conduit only needs to accommodate one cable at a time.

Track being laid on the lower section of the tramway. While part of the public highway, safety rules have meant that other vehicles are prohibited from using the road when the tramway is operating

The track on the lower section of tramway showing the hatches allowing access for maintenance of the guide pulleys on the curves.

The upper track, called the Great Orme Tramroad, is more like a cliff railway funicular. The running rails (flat bottom) are fixed to wooden sleepers and the cable runs on rollers between the rails; there is no conduit. Although the cable runs above the sleepers, the track is not fenced off. As the winding house is at the bottom of the upper section, it was necessary to attach a cable to the lower end of each car down to the winding house. There is another cable going up to the top of the funicular and round a pulley and back down to the other car. This allows the engine to pull the upper car down, which in turn pulls the lower car upwards. As the cables and its pulleys are above the ground there is sufficient space between the rails to accommodate them. The only parts protected from the public are the weighted point levers at the upper loop, which are covered by cages. This is the site of three accidents, in 1966, 2000 and 2009. On all occasions the collision was caused by a malfunction of the lower point.

The passing loop on the upper section of tramway, showing the difference the absence of a road makes to the construction of the line. In the photograph the point is set for tram number 7. When number 6 passes over it, the point will change and the figure 6 will be shown. Photograph by Trevor Service.

The initial cables were supplied by the St. Helen's Cable Company in 1902 and had to be hauled to the winding house using a team of twelve horses. The cable for the lower section was 1⅜ in diameter, while that on the upper section was ⅞ in diameter. The end of one cable was attached to one tramcar and it was lowered to Victoria Station, taking the cable through the conduit. It was attached to its winding drum and drawn back up to check that all was well. The second car was attached to its cable and the procedure repeated. Unlike the continuous cable tramways, on this funicular the cables are separate for each car. The two winding drums for a section are mounted on a common axle, but with the cables coiled opposite ways. So, as the drums turn together, one cable pays out while the other winds in.

The new winding house showing the drums for winding the lower section tramcars. There is a difference in the diameter on the drum of the wound cable compared to the unwound drum.

Both parts of the tramway are driven from a single winding house. This is located in the space between the two routes. When built, the winding house was equipped with a locomotive-type boiler providing the main steam power, with a small vertical boiler to top up the steam. Getting the boiler to the winding shed was not easy. A traction engine hauled a trailer carrying the boiler. When it reached the steep hill on the Great Orme, the trailer was held on the hill while the traction engine went forward paying out a cable. It was fitted with a winch and, once stationary, it winched the trailer and boiler up to itself. This was repeated until the boiler reached the winding house. Water for the boilers was provided from a Council reservoir built at the top of the hill in 1901. There were two steam engines built by C. and A. Musker in Liverpool, the engine for the upper tramway being 60 horsepower and that for the lower section 80 horsepower.

The Company ordered tramcars from Hurst, Nelson and Company in Motherwell. The Act authorising the tramway specified that the tramway could carry goods, minerals and parcels, but not animals. The Company clearly anticipated plenty of business from this quarter and the order to Hurst, Nelson included three (numbered 1 – 3) four-wheel goods vans called "Jockey Cars". They were used extensively in the building of the upper tramway, taking materials to the halfway station. However, the goods transport did not materialise, even though this included carrying coffins for burial at St Tudno's Church. In addition, there were four single-deck bogie passenger tramcars (numbered 4 – 7) that each seated 48 passengers with up to 12 standing. Car numbers 1 – 5 were delivered prior to the opening of the lower section in 1902 and the final two, 6 and 7, arrived in 1903 prior to the opening of the upper section. The side windows of the passenger cars were not glazed, though those in the bulkheads were. Instead, the side windows of numbers 4 and 5 had curtains, which from photographs appeared to be canvas, giving some protection in the rain. The curtains only lasted two years and then they were removed. This may have been connected with the seasonal opening of the tramway. In 1902 the lower section ran for the whole year, but is seems that this was not as successful as the Company had hoped and from 1903 the tramway only ran during the summer season. No doubt the Company then felt the curtains were unnecessary, showing a greater optimism in the North Wales weather than most. The speed for the lower section was 5 mph while the upper section ran at 7 mph.

Each tramcar was fitted with the usual handbrake acting on all wheels and a slipper brake acting on the track. Each braking system was operated by its own designated brake wheels. In addition, the cars on the lower section (numbers 4 and 5) had an emergency brake acting on the slot. A powerful spring was held back by the tension in the cable. If this tension ceased, for example if the cable broke, the spring drove cams that were forced out to rub against the sides of the slot. Unfortunately, it was found in operation that if there was a jerk as the cable was wound, the cable would slacken for a moment and the emergency brake would operate. It would then take four hours to release the brake and get the system moving again. Fed up with these interruptions, the Company allowed the engineers to disable the brake. A consequence of this action occurred in 1932 when the drawbar of tram number 5 broke and the tram ran away, with fatal results. This is examined in more detail later in this chapter. In the afternoons it became the practice for the driver of the descending upper-section car to tell the winchman how many passengers he had. If this was significantly greater than the number in the car at the halfway station, the winchman would instruct the driver to apply his hand brake to avoid the car running faster than the drum and hence being out of the winchman's control.

Tram number 4 on the lower section showing why no other vehicles are allowed to use the road while the tramway is working.

One unusual feature of the tramway in its early days was that, although being a cable-powered line, it was equipped with an overhead wire and the tramcars had trolley poles. This led to many thinking it was in fact an electric tramway. However, the overhead was a communications system and nothing to do with the power. Each tramcar was equipped with a telephone and a bell push (mounted on the platform roof) and the upper and lower tramways operated as independent

Number 5 at the old halfway station prior to its extensive rebuilding. Visitors are now able to view the winding house and see an historical exhibition about the tramway.

communications networks. On either tramway, the driver could speak to the other driver on his section and to the appropriate winchman. The bell was used to give instructions to the winchman. The procedure was that when the lower car driver was ready to leave, he would telephone the upper car driver to ask if he was also ready. Once he got a "yes" the lower car driver would ring two bells to tell the winchman to start. There were also bell codes to tell the winchman if any passengers had asked to alight at either intermediate stop. If there was any emergency, either driver would give a single bell and the winchman would immediately stop the cars. After a stop the drivers would check that the other was ready to move and then two bells were given by the ascending car to restart the journey. This system continued to be used until 1990 when it was replaced. This is described later in this chapter.

Once both sections of the tramway had opened, the directors were able to generate income and use this to develop their venture. The first addition was to build three tram sheds, one at each end of the upper line, and at the winding house for the lower line and a canopy for Victoria Station. Up to this point, when the tramway was not in use, the tramcars were parked at the end of their sections of line in the open. The sheds gave them protection from more serious weather (the car at the summit had been blown over several times during the winter months including 1917, 1922 and 1982), although the three jockey cars were still left in the open. Two were parked on sidings at the top of the lower section, by the winding house, while the third was dragged off the tracks at Victoria Station and left on the roadway.

In 1904 there was an argument between George White (the Manager) and the Directors, that resulted in his dismissal. Henry Sutcliffe was appointed in his place. In order to resolve the problem of the emergency brake, he had it removed and he also removed the overspeed governor that had been the cause of the jerky operation of the winding drums. The tramway operated well for the next years, though there were two minor collisions, one in 1909 and the other in 1911. There were no injuries or serious damage. In 1913 it was decided to replace the lower tramway engine as the existing one was not up to the job. A new 120 horsepower engine was purchased from the Sandicroft Foundry, Chester. This also allowed the old lower tramway 80 horsepower engine to take over the upper tramway and the 60 horsepower engine to be taken out and scrapped.

The tramway was popular and generated around 6% per annum in dividends for its shareholders. There was a downturn for 1918 when the tramway had to be closed as it needed a new cable and due to wartime restrictions was not able to get one until the following year, so lost many months of income.

On 21st August 1932 the drawbar on car number 5 snapped and the driver was able to bring the car to a halt using the handbrake. The same thing happened two days later to car number 4. This proved to be the worst crash in the history of the tramway. Car number 4 was descending the lower section from Ty-Gwyn Road into Old Road when the drawbar connecting it to the cable broke and the car ran away. The driver applied the handbrake and the slipper brake, but could not slow the car. It accelerated until reaching the curve at the top of Old Road where it left the rails and crashed into a stone wall. The driver and a 12 year-old girl, the daughter of an employee who worked at the winding house, standing next to him, died in the accident (at that time there was no restriction on passengers travelling on the same platform as the driver). The driver tried to save her by carrying her and jumping from the vehicle. Unfortunately, as he left the car it derailed and crashed against the stone wall, crushing them both. In addition, eleven passengers were hospitalised. The enquiry found that the crash had been caused by a combination of a change in the specification of the drawbar that was made of steel unsuitable for its purpose. It failed because of the sideways forces it encountered in use. In addition, the removal of the car's emergency brake meant there was no emergency back-up brake, allowing the tram to run away.

The upper terminus with the original car shed. This area has been developed since this photograph was taken, with a tea hut alongside where the tram stands and alongside the shed there is now a visitor centre.

The tramway was in a very difficult situation and passengers understandably wanted compensation. The Company had no cash reserves and their insurance Company had denied any liability. One passenger and his wife sued the tramway Company and the case was settled for £1,000 plus costs (the total amount claimed by the injured passengers was £14,000). However, they did not have this amount of money and had to file for bankruptcy. The County Bailiff put the tramway up for sale. The tramcars number 4 and 5 were fitted with new drawbars and emergency brakes. The new brakes relied on a governor such that if the tramcar's speed exceeded 6½ mph, it would activate four skids that had steel teeth that dug into the paved surface, bringing the car to a halt. As the track brake would have interfered with the efficiency of the new emergency brake it was removed from the two cars. A public demonstration showed that these were successful and the tramway reopened to the public on 17th May 1934, allowing the liquidator to offer the tramway as an operating concern.

GREAT ORME RAILWAYS LIMITED 1934 – 1949

It was sold in December 1934 to a group of mainly the existing shareholders for £5,600. They set up the Great Orme Railway Limited, registered in March 1935, and the new Company began operating the tramway. There was little change, other than the new name and a concession the new Company obtained from the Council that enabled them to run a service on Sundays.

When the new company took over in 1934 they renamed the system the Great Orme Railway and this was painted on the tramcars. It retained the railway name under Council ownership until 1977 when it was decided to revert back to the original tramway name.

LLANDUDNO URBAN DISTRICT COUNCIL (LATER ABERCONWY COUNTY COUNCIL THEN CONWY COUNTY COUNCIL) 1949 - DATE

In 1947 the Council decided to exercise their powers to compulsorily purchase the line. There was the usual argument about the price and the case ended up in court where a judgement was made of £8,407. The Council took over ownership on 1st January 1949. They opened it for the summer season in Easter of 1949. People were settling down after the hostilities and the overseas troops had been coming back home. People were ready for holidays and resorts like Llandudno were prepared to welcome them. The first year of Council operation generated income almost equivalent to the purchase price and the costs of improvements they had made. In the following years the income continued to rise, however so did the costs. Fare increases helped the situation.

In the same year, the RAF moved out of the summit hotel and it was put up for sale, as was the golf course. There was no interest and the golf course was eventually sold to a local farmer who

Victoria Station at the lower terminus was somewhat austere for much of its life. However, around the millennium, funding was obtained from the Heritage Lottery Fund and the European Union to refurbish and extend the facilities.

turned it back to sheep farming. The hotel was finally purchased by a syndicate including the boxer Randolph Turpin. The undertaking failed and Turpin was declared bankrupt with the hotel put up for sale. Llandudno Council purchased the building.

The Council decided in 1956 that the line could run at less cost if it was converted to electric operation. It was expected that the savings would be £1,400 per annum. A contract was signed with the English Electric Company to replace the steam power with electric motors and this was undertaken in the winter closure of 1957/58. An electricity sub-station was built and English Electric installed the controls and motors. The upper section is powered by a 75 hp motor and the lower section by a 125 hp motor. The steam engines were last used at the end of the 1957 season and the electric motors were used from the 1958 season. The journey time for the upper section is 4½ minutes and 5½ minutes for the lower section.

1963 saw an accident at the junction of Old Road and Ty-Gwyn Road. A driver of a motor car on the Ty-Gwyn Road ignored the warning and give-way signs and collided with a tramcar going up. Thankfully there were no injuries and just slight damage to the vehicles, but it was a wake-up call about the dangers of the crossing, though it took nearly 30 years before any action was taken to make the junction safer. I had a similar experience around the millennium when riding up the lower section of tramway. A motor car cut across the front of the tram I was travelling in, forcing the driver to hit the emergency button and halt the journey. He then got on his radio to report the registration number of the errant car driver. Although the tramcar halted very suddenly there were no injuries to the passengers or driver.

In 1965 passengers waiting for trams at the summit were given some comfort as a brick shelter was built enabling protection from adverse weather. In 1966 there was a precursor to later serious accidents when in August the tramcars on the upper section collided at the passing loop. The lower point malfunctioned and the rear bogie of the ascending car took the wrong direction. Damage was slight and there were no injuries. The cars and line were repaired in a few days and the service continued. However, this point was to cause similar problems some 34 years later.

In 1973 there was a promotion featuring the narrow gauge railways of Wales under the title "Great Little Trains of Wales", encouraging visitors to the railways and with each railway helping publicise the others. The Great Orme Tramway featured in the publication, bringing more visitors to travel on it.

Changes in the local authority boundaries in 1974 meant that the Llandudno Urban District Council was taken over by the new Aberconwy Borough Council. In 1977 it was determined that the name should revert to the original Great Orme Tramway in commemoration of its 75th anniversary. This was followed five years later, on 31st July 1982, by the 80th anniversary celebrations. Unfortunately, the number of passengers travelling on the line had dropped over the years and the line was running at a loss. The situation was not helped on 27th September when tramcar number 7 was blown over by high winds when at the summit. It took several days to effect repairs and re-open the upper tramway.

At the summit station tramcar number 7 was caught in high winds one night and was blown over, causing damage to itself and the tramway.

It was also becoming clear that the infrastructure of the tramway required renewal. The Council seriously thought about leasing the tramway to Bolton Trams Limited, a heritage tramway Company, however this did not take place, possibly because the lawyers discovered that the original Act of 1898 did not allow the Council to lease the line. In 1989 the Railway Inspectorate indicated that it was likely to close the tramway on safety grounds at the following year's inspection if remedial work had not been undertaken. Aberconwy Council had a trading department called Grŵp Aberconwy and it was decided to let them manage the tramway with a five-year business plan and a £405,000 investment programme. The programme was started in the winter of 1989/90. The track of the upper section was relayed with heavier section rail (apart from the loop), new sleepers and new cables. The refurbished upper section re-opened on 28th June 1990. Another improvement was on communications where the old overhead line and telephones were replaced by radio, following a break in the overhead line. Inspection showed that the overhead wire was badly worn and needed replacing. It was decided to replace that system of communications with a radio control system. Airlink of Llandudno equipped the cars and winding house. The system incorporated a Dead Man's pedal, meaning the system would shut down if the driver removed his foot from the pedal. This gave the opportunity to cease having a conductor on the trams. As the old system relied on the trolley pole remaining in contact with the wire, the conductor's job was to keep a check on it and replace it immediately should it dewire. The Ministry of Transport were concerned that operating tramcars with open platforms and no conductor was unsafe. It requested that waist-height doors be fitted that would be closed when the tramcar was moving. This was done by Sutton Engineering of Llandudno. The Ministry of Transport approved the changes and the tramcars were now crewed by just the driver, making significant staffing savings.

It was decided in the 1990/1 winter to refurbish the tramway. The tramcars were given a new blue and gold livery and staff were issued with smart blue and gold uniforms. Victoria Station was given a tea garden and the tickets redesigned making them a souvenir of the journey.

During the1991/2 winter closure of the tramway, tramcar number 7 was taken away from the tramway to be repaired at Grŵp Aberconwy's Llandudno workshops. It returned in readiness for the 1992 season. Also in 1992 the tramcars were given names of local North Wales saints. They were no. 4 St Tudno; no. 5 St Silio; no. 6 St Seiriol; and no. 7 St. Trillo. There was another change at the top of Old Road into Ty-Gwyn Road where traffic lights, triggered by transponders under the track, had been erected to give priority to the trams and make the junction safer.

Tramcars numbers 6 and 7 passing at the upper section loop. By now the overhead wire had been removed and the trolley poles are permanently set in the down position.

A new station and visitor centre were built at the summit terminus in 1992, the year of the tramway's 90th anniversary. The following year saw very heavy rain around many parts of the British Isles, including the Great Orme. The flooding swept down the tramway line causing damage to the track and track bed forcing the tramway to close. W. Hocking & Co. Ltd of Cardiff helped the tramway repair the track-work. The tramway re-opened on 2nd July.

Local government was reorganised again in 1996 and the new owners of the tramway became the new Conwy County Council. Two years later, in 1998, there was another accident when a problem on the upper section meant a replacement bus service was used. The driver thought that the whole line had closed and so he took his load of passengers down Old Road, only to meet a tramcar going up. The bus failed to stop in time and it hit the tramcar.

The new millennium brought more problems for the tramway. The upper loop became the site of another accident. The tramway opened a few days before Easter and the drivers immediately reported that the lower point was occasionally failing to be thrown over by the descending car, meaning that, unless the point was changed by hand, it would direct the car onto the wrong side (looking uphill, car 6 always takes the right hand side and car 7 the left hand side) and into the path of the other car. When the point had failed to change, the driver would tell the winding house to stop the cars and manually change the point. It was realised that on Easter Sunday and Monday this would be too restrictive for the service frequency expected. It was decided to place an employee at the point to check its operation and change it by hand if it failed to operate correctly.

The upper terminal buildings opened in 1992. Prior to this the tramcars would halt outside the old shed, meaning passengers alighted in the open. Now the trams enter the covered area giving shelter to visitors in inclement weather.

The accident occurred on Easter Sunday afternoon when car 7 took the wrong loop and collided with car 6. Both drivers recognised the danger and both pressed their emergency halt button. The communications system could not cope with two signals at the same time and jammed both of them. The first the winchman knew of the problem was when the cables tightened, by which time the cars had collided. A second factor that did not help were the cable tensioning devices. The reason for this is that the speed at which the cable moves varies during the operation. Both the cars have separate cables going from the car to the winding house, each with its own winding drum. These are both mounted on the same shaft, so turn at the same rate. However, as the cable is paid out or wound on, the working diameter changes; it is larger when full of cable and smaller when empty. As the two upper cars are joined by the cable going up to the upper terminus, they have to travel at the same speed. To allow for the changes in drum diameter there are cable tensioning devices in the winding house. Each cable passes over a hole and the cable loops down into the hole with a heavy weight keeping it tensioned. In an emergency, when the motor was stopped, the momentum of the cars would keep them moving, using the slack in the cable, until the tensioning weight reached the end of its movement, when the cable would stop. On this occasion this was all too late as the collision had already occurred.

Of the 40 passengers in each car 17 people were injured. Her Majesty's Railway Inspectorate carried out an investigation and made a report. It was clear that neither the temporary attendant or the tram driver noticed the error. The driver had been driving car 6 all morning, then had a break followed by taking car 7 for the afternoon. The Inspector felt that this may have been one factor causing the accident. Although the point lever on the lower point displayed the number of the car it was set for, the driver said on approaching the point he could not see the number because the attendant blocked his view. He also said that the point looked correctly set. It was felt that he may have been confused by the point blade setting, having got used to it with car 6 and forgot he was on car 7. The attendant, who was normally part of the security team, said his instructions were to check the point blade was snug against the stock rail and he was not checking that it was set for the correct side of the loop, that was the responsibility of the driver. The conclusion of the Inspector was that the cause of the collision was inadequate staff training. He issued a prohibition notice until a proper staff training programme had been implemented. The tramway also decided to carry out repair work on the point, so the upper section was closed for repairs.

During this time the lower section also had a problem and shut the whole tramway down for what transpired to be over a year. A replacement bus service was operated during this time.

As it happened, the winding house was reconstructed (it re-opened on 20th September 2001). A new control and communications system from Doppelmayr was installed. Using inductive loop technology, the winding engineer is now able to see the exact position of each tramcar. The closure also enabled the tramway to give a complete refurbishment to the mechanical parts of all the tramcars. With an almost completely new tramway it reached its centenary on 31st July 2002 and the occasion was celebrated with invited guests and the town band. The day saw over 1,000 passengers joining in the event. The track of the lower section was replaced over several years, including the winters of 2002/3, 2003/4 and 2004/5 and there was also an extension to the buildings at Victoria Station.

There was a minor collision with an Arriva bus in July 2007. In 2008 the Engineer for the insurance underwriter advised the tramway to undertake repairs to the points on the upper section. During the closed winter season, the Council chose to replace the whole loop and points and offered the contract to a track-laying company. Before the tramway re-opened at Easter, the work was inspected by the insurers and HM Railway Inspectors. They discovered that the new track was unsuitable for cable operation. The tramway immediately put remedial work in hand, but in the time available this was the bare minimum.

An accident occurred on 15th September 2009 on the upper section after the trams had completed seven journeys. Tram 7 approached the loop from the summit and tram 6 from the halfway station. As tram 6 passed over the lower point, its front bogie followed the correct path, but the rear bogie took the wrong direction and the tram straddled the two tracks. Both drivers saw the danger and hit their emergency stop buttons, while the winch engineer watched the movement on closed circuit television also saw the back of tram 6 take the wrong direction and he operated his emergency stop button. Both drivers also applied their brakes but the tramcars collided. There were 40 people in tram 6 and 24 people in tram 7. Although shaken only one person was hurt and that was a minor injury. Buses were brought in to take the passengers down to Victoria Station. The Rail Accident Investigation Branch instituted an investigation. It was found that the tramcars had not stopped immediately due to a one-second delay in the operation of the emergency stop and the take-up of slack in the cable tensioning devices (as detailed in the 2000 collision).

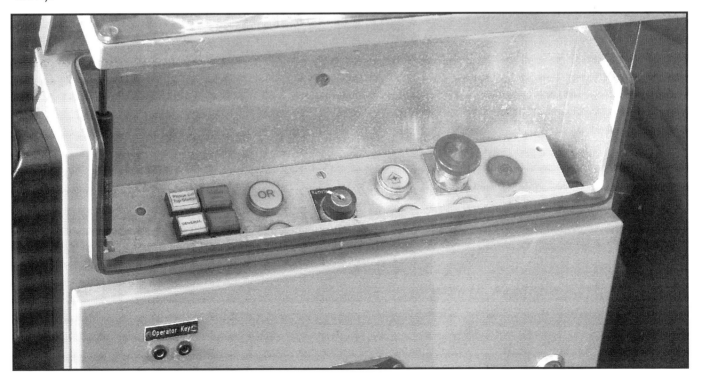

The communications panel fitted on each end of the tramcars. This enables the driver to signal to the other driver and the winding man. They can also speak via mobile telephones.

The consequence of tramcar number 6 splitting the lower points of the upper loop was the collision with number 7. Fortunately no one was badly hurt and of the 40 people involved only one received a minor injury, though all were shaken.

The conclusions of the investigation were that the point had changed position as the leading bogie of car 6 had gone over it, misdirecting the rear bogie. The movement of the front bogie had set up forces that moved the blades, throwing the lever over to the wrong position. The cause was wear and degradation of the point. They recommended a proper regime of inspection and maintenance. The upper section of the tramway was closed. Remedial work was carried out on the upper loop and, after some trial running, the tramway re-opened on 20th March 2010 for the summer season.

There was another incident on 22nd March 2015 when a tram running along Old Road collided with a parked car. Normally the tramway runs from 1st April to 31st October and during that time road vehicles are prohibited from parking in the road. However, the tramway wanted to undertake trial runs before the season started. They said that they had informed residents living in the road that they should not park cars for the fortnight before the 1st April. The car owner claimed that these had never been sent. The tramcar going up the hill had only one person aboard, the driver. It collided with the car causing minor damage to its front offside wing. The tramway opened as usual on 1st April.

In 2012 the tramway celebrated its 110th birthday. It is unique, as in 2017 it is the only tramway from the Victorian era continuing to operate with all its original passenger tramcars. The whole passenger fleet has given service for 114 years and looks like it will continue for many more.

THE TRAMWAY FLEET

GREAT ORME TRAMWAYS 1902 - DATE

Fleet number	Date built	Builder	Type	Number of seats
1 – 3	1902	Hurst, Nelson and Co Ltd †	Van Jockey car	0
4 and 5	1902	Hurst, Nelson and Co Ltd ‡	Single deck, bogie	48
6 and 7	1903	Hurst, Nelson and Co Ltd ‡	Single deck, bogie	48

Notes

† Withdrawn circa 1920

‡ Since 1992 the tramcars have been named:

    4 St Tudno

    5 St Silio

    6 St Seiriol

    7 St Trillo

Livery

All deep yellow, later all blue, then blue and white with various shades of blue.

REFERENCES

North Wales Tramways, by K. Turner, 1979, David and Charles

Great Orme Tramway – the first 80 years by R. C. Anderson, 1982, Light Rail Transit Association

By Tram to the Summit, by P. M. Smith, 1983, North Wales Tramway Museum Association

Great Orme Tramway, by R. Sutton, 1992, Grŵp Aberconwy

Great Orme Tramways, Tramway and Railway World, 9th October 1902

The Funicular Revival: Part 4 – Great Orme, by J. H. Price, 1994, Light Railway and Modern Tramway

North Wales Transport, by J. Roberts, 1998, Sutton Publishing

Great Orme Tramway Centenary, by J. Firbank, 2002, Conwy County Borough Council

The Great Orme Tramway – Over a Century of Service, by Keith Turner, 2003, Gwasg Carreg Gwalch

Collision on the Great Orme Tramway, 15th September 2009, RAIB 2010

Tramcar number 6 showing the cable attachments under the car. This is one of the upper section trams and so is attached to two cables. The lower one is attached to the cable running from the winding house while the other is attached to the cable connecting both trams via the upper terminus pulley.

CHAPTER 11

AFTERWORD

The development of cable traction for street tramways came at a time of great change of public transport for the masses. The precursor to public road transport was probably the use of farm carts to take villagers to markets or fairs in nearby towns. Transport that ran to a rudimentary timetable was the stage coach, becoming more reliable with mail coaches. The first town transport to run to a regular route and timetable was the horse omnibus. In Britain, the first horse bus (as opposed to coach) was introduced by George Shillibeer after he had introduced similar vehicles in Paris in 1827. His novel idea for London was to use the vehicle on a fixed route and pick-up passengers and charge them fares to ride. He started his service in 1829, but fares were high and the poorer people could not afford to travel. One of the main problems was that the streets were in a dreadful state, deep in mud in the wet and full of dust in the dry.

The low rolling resistance of steel wheels on steels rails, already exploited by the railways, led to street tramways with horses being able to haul larger vehicles with more passengers than horse buses. As the early tramways usually made a good profit for the investors, there was a boom in the number being built in towns but, as more tramways opened, so the high running costs became an issue. Horses got tired and generally the operators needed three sets of horses for each tramcar for each day, as opposed to staff who worked 12-hour days. So the search was on for a cheaper motive power. Around the 1880s, cheaper motive power was needed but there was no obvious replacement for the horse at this time. Main choices were steam power, electric or cable but there were also forays using clockwork, gas, petrol, compressed air and diesel.

The Ferry Landings terminus on the San Francisco Market Street cable tramway.
This photograph was taken at the height of the popularity of cable street tramways.

Steam power in the form of small locomotives was the first solution. These diminutive engines could haul large double deck passenger tramcars and were more economic to run than horse trams. The main disadvantage for operators considering changing over from horse to steam tram was the need to relay the track in order that it could carry the weight of the locomotives and heavier tramcars. In addition there was some reluctance by the more affluent residents to this form of transport. They were able to influence the law to require that the locomotives be disguised as anonymous boxes, showing no moving parts so as not to scare their horses. The locomotives were also required to consume their own smoke, leading to many complaints if a driver should produce fumes.

A Birmingham Central Tramways Company steam tram, showing the box-like covering for the locomotive required by law. The engine could haul a much larger tramcar than horses at much less cost. In addition the Tramways Acts stated that the locomotive had to consume its own smoke, in other words be smoke free, hence the condensing tubes on the roof.

After Andrew Smith Hallidie had demonstrated the practicability of cable tramways on the Clay Street line in San Francisco, many promotors looked to cables as the solution to the tramway power problem. However, there were two significant financial issues that had to be addressed. The first was insurmountable; the high initial costs of building the tramway. To run a cable tramway it was necessary to dig a trench the full length of each track to build the conduit carrying the cable under the road surface. Not only did the conduit have to be built so as to contain the cable, no matter the twists and changes of level of the road, but it also needed to be strong enough to withstand the pounding it got from the other road traffic. Whilst most horse traffic was relatively light, there were also traction engines that hauled heavily-loaded trailers. Frequently, the tramway track had the best road surface with the remainder being left as muddy quagmires and road traffic would head for the tram track as it gave a smoother surface to travel on. Under the restrictive British law the maintenance of the road between and for 18 inches either side of the rails lay entirely with the tramway operator. This was in addition to the requirement to pay rates on the area covered by tramway track. Even today this is noticeable where at junctions the tramway points may be built with the blades some distance in advance of the frog. The reason is to keep the blade, a potentially weak place of the point, on a straight section of road to avoid the stresses of turning cars and lorries.

In the early 1880s the electric motor was very much in its infancy. Indeed, the first demonstration of an electric locomotive was given in the 1850s and for many years the early motors had insufficient power to climb hills. No doubt many extravagant claims were being made for the electric motor which were not being achieved in reality. It can be imagined that an investor may have been deterred by the still-experimental electric motor compared to the proven cable system, as well as being able to understand a tramcar being pulled by a cable, while electricity was an alien concept.

The cable system was particularly attractive in towns with steep hills. The cable could haul tramcars up slopes that were impractical for horses and that would be a major challenge for steam locomotives. It is no coincidence that in Britain cable power was most usually chosen for routes with steep hills. However, this advantage did not last long. Developments in electric motor technology advanced very quickly and, by the end of the 19th century it was becoming clear that electricity was the most economic, and hence profitable, means of powering tramways. The difference in costs was very significant, with the cable system being by far more expensive than electric power (though much cheaper than the horse). One of the costliest factors was the cable. The manufacturers would claim that their cable had a working life of twelve to eighteen months. In reality the cables would need replacing far more frequently. It was reported that some of the San Francisco systems were replacing their cable every ten weeks. The cost of the cable was high and the tramway would be out of action for many hours while the old cable was removed and replaced by the new cable. If the need to replace was an emergency rather than a planned night-time operation, there would be a considerable loss of income as well. The impact of the electric tramway on the cable systems was profound. This was particularly so as reluctant Councils were persuaded to agree to having overhead wires erected in their streets (many of whom rapidly changed their minds when they became tramway operators and the significant cost savings of electricity became most persuasive).

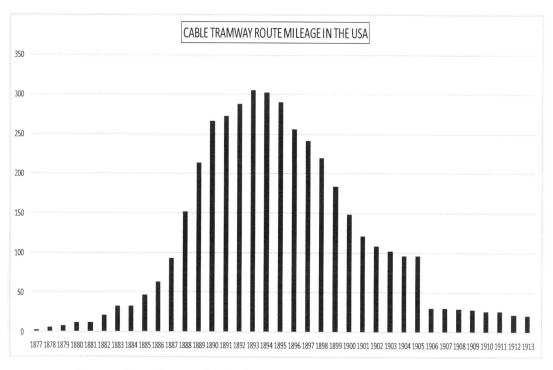

Above: The rise and fall of cable street tramways in the USA

The effect of the development of electric technology is best demonstrated by the graph showing the changes in the operating mileage of cable tramways in the USA over a 36 year period from 1877 to 1913. The mileage rises from close to zero to a peak of just over 300 in 1893 and back to around 20 in 1913. Whilst this shows the situation in the USA the picture in Britain was very similar. It was distorted because there were relatively small numbers of cable systems and the largest British cable tramway, the Edinburgh system with its over 25 miles of cable tramway, lasted far longer than the world average. The Edinburgh cable tramway ran from 1888 to 1923, some 35 years. The table compares the life of all the British cable street tramways.

Below: A summary of all the cable street tramways operated in the British Isles

WORKING LIFE	TRAMWAY	YEAR OPEN	YEAR CLOSED
19 years	Highgate Hill	1884	1909
35 years	Edinburgh	1888	1923
23 years	Birmingham	1888	1911
12 years	Brixton Hill	1892	1904
34 years	Matlock	1893	1927
33 years	Upper Douglas	1896	1929
3 years	Swansea, Constitution Hill	1898	1901
114+ years	Great Orme	1902	Date

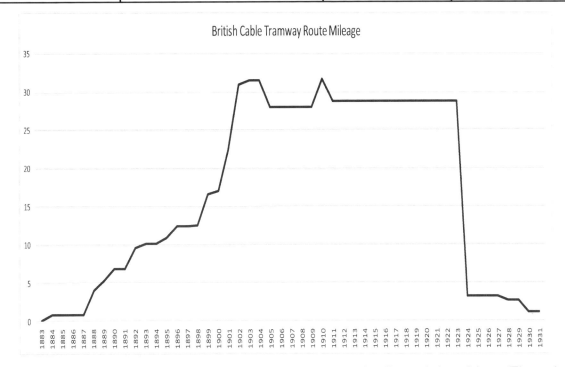

British Cable Tramway Route Mileage

The cable street tramway was not the expected solution to the financial problem. The advantages and economies of electric power overtook the initial benefits of cable and it soon became clear that cable trams were in decline. Today very few cable street tramways have survived. Most famous are those in San Francisco, where three routes run in the city and are a popular tourist attraction. There is another in Wellington, New Zealand and, of course, the Great Orme Tramway in North Wales.

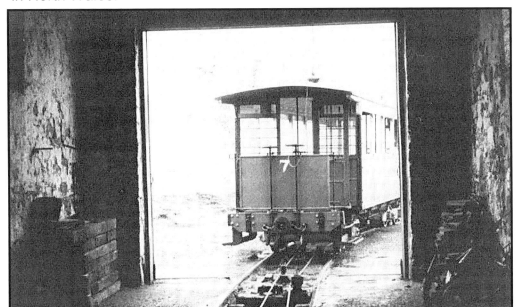

The end of the line. The old upper tramcar shed on the Great Orme Tramway. Since this photograph was taken in the 1960s the whole terminus complex has been rebuilt to incorporate a visitor centre and give shelter to patrons in inclement weather.

APPENDIX

CABLE TRAMWAY INNOVATORS

BROOKS, BENJAMIN H. 1842 - 1931

The first trailblazer actually played a very small part in the development of street cable tramways but it was to have profound consequences. Benjamin Brooks was a San Francisco attorney who became interested in street cable tramways. He gathered some associates of a like mind, C.S. Bushnell, Abner Doubleday and E.W. Steele. They had plans to build a long system from the San Francisco town centre to Cow Hollow and in 1870 obtained a franchise from the city authorities to build the line. Brooks, and an engineer W.H. Hepburn, set about designing the cable system. This included some of the main features of future cable tramways, such as the use of a stationary engine to drive an endless cable located under the road surface with a grip on the tramcars enabling the tram to attach to the cable or to be released. However, Brooks and his associates were unable to find the necessary funding. Brooks and Hepburn did not patent their developments, possibly because no one would provide financial backing and would have expressed doubt as to whether it was a practical proposition. They decided to sell the franchise and Andrew S. Hallidie purchased it for $2,000 in 1869.

BUCKNALL SMITH, J.

J. Bucknall Smith worked for some time in the Chief Engineer's Department of The Cable Tramways Company. In 1883 the Highgate Hill tramway approached him to work with William Eppelsheimer as Constructing Engineers on the building of the tramway, as they had been let down by W. W. Hanscom, the initial choice. In 1887 he used his knowledge and experience to write the authoritative book "A Treatise Upon Cable Or Rope Traction, As Applied to the Working of Street and Other Railways"

CASEBOLT, HENRY 1816 - 1892

Henry Casebolt was an entrepreneur who built carriages and tramcars. He promoted the Sutter Street line in San Francisco, then a horse tramway. Having seen the success of the Clay Street cable line he proposed, in 1876, that the Sutter Street line should adopt cable power. However, discussions with Hallidie were not fruitful. Hallidie demanded Royalties of £50,000 per annum for use of the patents, plus more royalties for using the grip design. Casebolt refused and enlisted his Engineer Asa Hovey to design a grip that did not use any Hallidie patents. It was a side grip with a lever operation, rather than a wheel and it was so successful that other cable tramways used it. The conversion to cable operation led to claims and counterclaims over patent infringement. Casebolt sold his interest in the Sutter Street line in 1880.

COLAM, WILLIAM NEWBY 1853 - 1930

William Newby Colam was an Engineer who was involved in the supervision of the Highgate Hill tramway with William E. Eppelsheimer, both of whom worked for Patent Cable Tramways Corporation. The line was completed in 1884 and Newby Colam presented a paper on cable tramways

to the Society of Engineers in 1885 in London. After the turbulent period caused by the bankruptcy of the Steep Grade Company in 1886 and the change of ownership several times, the line closed for four years after 1892. It was purchased by the Highgate Hill Tramways Limited in 1896 with William Newby Colam as the Engineer and Manager. Following repairs required by the Board of Trade he obtained the necessary permission to reopen the line in 1897. From 1884 he was the Designer and Consultant Engineer for the Edinburgh Northern Cable Tramways. He was also appointed in 1890 as Design Engineer for the Brixton Hill and Matlock Cable Tramways.

He presented several papers on the subject to the Society of Municipal and Sanitary Engineers, including one in 1885 titled "Cable Tramways", and one to the Society of Municipal and County Engineers in 1890 titled "Edinburgh Northern Cable Tramways", by which time he was Vice President of the Society (becoming President the following year). He also presented a paper to the Society of Municipal and County Engineers in 1898 entitled "Conversion of Edinburgh, Leith and Portobello Horse Tramways Systems into Cable Traction"

DOUBLEDAY, ABNER 1819 - 1893

Abner Doubleday was a career officer in the United States Army. Between 1869 and 1871 he was based in San Francisco. During this period he joined with Benjamin H. Brooks to build a cable tramway in the City. In 1870 they obtained a franchise to build a line, however nothing came of the idea and they sold the franchise to Hallidie. It has been said that Doubleday patented the cable street tramway and built the first line. He did not, having been moved by the army to Texas in 1871.

EPPELSHEIMER, WILLIAM E. 1842 - ?

William E. Eppelsheimer was born in what is present-day Germany and trained as an engineer. From 1873 he worked with Andrew Smith Hallidie to design and build the world's first street cable tramway. While Hallidie's name is most associated with the invention of the street cable tramway, Eppelsheimer played a significant and important part. This is illustrated by his career after the Clay Street line. He designed a more practical grip than the Hallidie version originally used on the line. It was Eppelsheimer's design that was also used on other tramways in San Francisco and other cities. He designed the Chicago City Railway, a cable tramway that opened in 1882. In 1884 he travelled to England and was the replacement Engineer for the Highgate Hill Tramway when the original Engineer failed to meet his targets.

GARDNER, ELEAZER S.

Eleazer S. Gardner, a native of Philadelphia, was granted a patent in 1858 for "Improvements in Tracks for City Railways", which set out the main principles required for cable propulsion in town streets. However, he did not implement his ideas although there is a view that he used them when cable tramways were built in Philadelphia in 1883. The patent was somewhat lacking in detail, outlining only the principal aspects.

GILLHAM, ROBERT 1854 - 1899

Robert Gillham was the author of "Cable Railways: Their History, and Use in America", published in 1889.

HALLIDIE, ANDREW SMITH 1836 - 1900

Andrew Smith Hallidie was born Andrew Smith in London, England on 16th March 1836 and his parents were Scottish. His father was an inventor with a speciality in wire ropes. He grew up learning engineering from his father but at the age of 16 his health deteriorated. In 1852 his father took him to California to live in a more congenial climate. His father returned to England after a year but Andrew Smith stayed on, joining the gold rush in California, first as a prospector then as a surveyor and blacksmith. Around this time he changed his name by adding the surname Hallidie in honour of his uncle and godfather Sir Andrew Hallidie who had been royal physician to King William IV and then Queen Victoria. In 1857 he moved to San Francisco and opened a wire rope factory, A. S. Hallidie & Co., renamed the California Wire Works in 1883 with Hallidie as President. The Company was taken over by Washburn and Moen Manufacturing Company in 1895. He was active in promoting the use of wire rope, including for building suspension bridges and for hauling ore cars out of mines. In November 1863 he married Martha Elizabeth Woods and then on 4th January 1864 he formally became a United States citizen, actually using his birth name of Andrew Smith.

There is an unconfirmed story that one wet day, in 1869, he was standing with a friend in San Francisco and they saw a horse-drawn tramcar climbing the steep hill. The horses slipped and were dragged back by the weight of the tramcar. His friend turned to him and asked "Andrew, why don't you go to work and invent something to pull street cars safely up steep grades and prevent such accidents?" His business and experience with cable hauling of mining wagons led him to explore the use of cable haulage for street tramways. The key feature of the cable tramway system is an endless wire cable that is continuously moving. Hallidie had previously developed an endless ropeway for carrying ore in buckets for the mining industry. He improved the quality of the cable by twisting six smaller cables that each contained nineteen steel wires. This upgraded cable was more flexible and less prone to breakage (it had a tensile strength of 160,000 pounds per square inch), and was capable of being frequently bent and straightened without it breaking.

He vested all his patents in the Cable Railway Company, of which he was president. The Company purchased other cable tramway patents and developed a virtual monopoly over the technology. The aim of the Company was to profit from these patents and similar Companies were set up in other countries developing cable tramways. As a result Hallidie became very rich, although, in doing so, the cost of constructing new lines increased. While he took an interest in cable tramway development in Britain he did not become personally involved in the design or building of any.

Hallidie continued to live in San Francisco and took an active part in the community including being president of the local Mechanics Institute. He tried his hand at politics, standing for Mayor and as member of the California State Senate, but he failed to be elected. He died at the age of 65 at his San Francisco residence and was buried at Laurel Hill Cemetery (later relocated to Cyprus Lawn Cemetery).

HANSCOM, WILLIAM WALLACE ? - ?

William Wallace Hanscom was a cable tramway Engineer in San Francisco. He was author of a book "Cable Propulsion" published in the "Transactions of the Technical Society of the Pacific Coast" 1884. He advertised in the American Railroad Journal in 1885. He wrote an article on "Cable Railway Propulsion" in the July 1886 issue of The Street Railway Gazette.

HOVEY, ASA E. 1830 - ?

Asa Hovey was the Engineer for the Sutter Street line under the management of Henry Casebolt where he was employed as a Master Mechanic and Inventor. When Henry Casebolt sought to avoid having to pay high royalty fees to Hallidie, he worked with Hovey to design a side grip operated by levers. This proved to be so effective that it became the most commonly used grip by cable tramways. He was also hired to design the Chicago City Railway, the first cable tramway in America that was outside San Francisco.

HUTCHINSON, CHARLES SCROPE (MAJOR GENERAL) 1826 - 1912

Major General Hutchinson was the Board of Trade Inspector of Railways who undertook visits to tramways to determine their suitability for public operation.

KINCAID, JOSEPH 1834 - 1907

In his mid-20s Joseph Kincaid worked for Charles Blacker Vignoles (who proposed using a flat bottom rail on the London and Croydon Railway that became known as the Vignoles rail). In 1879 he built the Dublin Southern District Tramways Company horse-car line from Dublin to Black Rock. He was dissatisfied with the rail then available and he designed grooved rails that fitted on cast iron chairs embedded in concrete. He was involved in the Highgate Hill Cable Tramway. Later, he worked with Edward Pritchard, as joint Consulting Engineers for the Birmingham Central Tramways cable line. In 1892 he joined fellow Engineers to form what was to become Kincaid, Walter, Manville and Dawson, Consulting Engineers.

MACKENZIE, WILLIAM (SIR) 1849 - 1923

Sir William Mackenzie was born near Peterborough in Canada. After working as a teacher and sawmill manager, he became a contractor working under James Ross working on railway projects in Canada and America. He and James Ross became partners and purchased the Toronto tramway in 1891. In 1896 he and James Ross set up the City of Birmingham Tramways Company that acquired the bankrupt Birmingham Central Tramways Company with the aim of converting the horse, accumulator and cable lines to electric operation. Later he built much of the Canadian Northern Railway. He was knighted in 1911 for his contribution to the railway industry. He died in 1923 in Ontario.

MARKS, GEORGE CROYDON (SIR) 1858 - 1938

Sir George Croydon Marks developed his career working for Sir Richard Tangye, whose company built, among other machinery, funicular cliff lifts. As Head of the Lift Department, Marks supervised the construction of the Saltburn cliff lift. He then set up his own Company and became involved in the erection of a number of funiculars. One was the Swansea Constitution Hill cable tramway. However, this was the only cable operated street tramway he was associated with.

MORE, JAMES ? - ?

James More was the engineer working for Dick, Kerr and Company when they built the Upper Douglas Cable Tramway. It was his responsibility to design the driving gear, terminal and conduit pulleys and the winding house and depot buildings.

MARINDIN, FRANCIS ARTHUR, (MAJOR SIR) 1838 - 1900

Major Sir Francis Marindin joined the army as an ensign in 1854. He became famous for founding the Royal Engineers Football team in 1869, which won the FA cup in 1875. In the same year he became the President of the Football Association and an Inspector for the Board of Trade. He rose to become Senior Inspector of Railways. He undertook the second inspection of the Swansea Constitution Hill tramway after the line had failed its first inspection.

NEWNES, GEORGE (SIR) 1851 - 1910

Sir George Newnes was born in Matlock and in 1881 he founded the magazine "Tit-Bits". In 1891 he added "The Strand Magazine" to his publications and regularly printed Sherlock Holmes stories. At the same time, he founded George Newnes Limited, a publishing company. He built a large house in Lynton in 1887 and this coincided with the proposal to build a water-powered cliff funicular to connect Lynton with Lynmouth. He was approached by Thomas Hewitt to help fund the project. Newnes agreed and became a director of the funicular that opened in 1890. Newnes kept in contact with his home town of Matlock and heard about the proposal to build a cable tramway. Newnes approached the promotors and offered to fund the line. No doubt his confidence in this type of transport was high due to the success of the Lynton funicular. The Matlock cable tramway opened in 1893. He was also influential in the construction of the Lynton and Barnstable Railway that opened in 1898.

PRITCHARD, EDWARD 1838 – 1900

Edward Pritchard was a Civil Engineer working on the design and construction of waterworks and sewage farms. In 1885 he joined with Joseph Kincaid to be the Consulting Engineers for the Birmingham Central Tramways cable line.

ROBINSON, JAMES CLIFTON (SIR) 1848 - 1910

Sir James Clifton Robinson is more associated with his role as general manager of the London United Tramways, overseeing the electrification of the system and then managing it for 16 years. However, an incident when managing the Los Angeles Cable Railway almost led to the end of his career in tramway management. His involvement with tramways started at an early age for him and at the beginning of tramways in Britain and Europe. At the age of 12 he saw the first horse street tramway operating in Birkenhead and immediately decided this was the career for him. He managed to gain employment as an office boy for George Francis Train. The two got on very well and some of the bravado and showmanship of Train rubbed off on Robinson. In 1862 he was sent to establish and manage the Staffordshire Potteries Street Railway, the latest venture of Train. In 1866 he travelled to America with Train where he was involved in helping in the development of many horse tramways. He returned to Britain in 1871 working for Fisher and Parrish, railway and tramway contractors. He was involved in tramways in London, Liverpool and Dublin. In 1873 he was appointed General Manager of the Cork tramways. He moved to the Bristol Tramways Company in 1875 and then to Edinburgh Street Tramways in 1882. He was interested in replacing horse power with mechanical power. He wrote and had published a paper on cable traction that he presented to the Royal Society of Arts in 1883. As a result, he was invited to take on the management of the Highgate Hill tramway. From 1884 to 1886 he became General Manager of the Patent Cable Tramways Corporation Limited (owners of the Highgate line).

Returning to America in 1887 he took on the management of the Los Angeles Cable Railway. In 1889 there was a flood that swept sand and debris into the cable conduit. He worked his men hard to clear the mess and get the system running again. He was chided by a friend on the closing of the system so he did something reminiscent of George Train. He bet his friend a cigar that the trams would be running by 1.00 p.m. the next day. In order to win he ordered the winding house engines to be started and some cars to run. The conduit had not been completely cleared and the rubbish in them caused expensive damage to the system. As a consequence, he and the cable tramway parted company. His future in tramways seemed bleak. However, in that year the American Street Railway Association had asked him to report on mechanical traction for street tramways. He toured the world comparing horse, cable and electric traction in many countries. His report titled "A Report of the Committee on a Year's Progress of Cable Motive Power" was presented in 1891 and this went a long way in re-establishing his reputation. Also while compiling the report he had started to feel that the future of tramways lay with electric power.

He returned to Britain in 1891 to become Managing Director of the Imperial Tramways Company, owners of the Dublin Southern, Gloucester, Middlesbrough and Reading tramways and the Corris Railway. The Company also acquired the Bristol tramway and Robinson was charged with converting it to electrical operation.

In 1894 the London United Tramways Company was formed that purchased the West Metropolitan Tramways Company with the intention of converting it from horse power to electric. They appointed Robinson as Managing Director and Engineer and he worked with George White to achieve the conversion. He continued to be a larger than life character. He had a large house (Garrick Villa, formerly occupied by David Garrick, actor and theatre manager) in Hampton that was on one of the LUT tram routes. Robinson had a siding laid from the tramway into his garden and he also had his personal, highly decorated, tramcar. King Edward knighted him in 1905 for his services in developing tramway and railway systems in London. He continued to run the company for 16 years finally resigning in 1910.

He had considerable business interests throughout his life as a Consultant on public transport matters. Later in 1910 he visited America as part of this work. On 6th November 1910 he was travelling back to his hotel in a tramcar with his wife when he had a seizure and died within a few minutes.

ROOT, HENRY 1845 - ?

Henry Root was a railway engineer on the Central and Southern Pacific Railroad who, in 1876, was recruited to build the California Street Cable Railroad. He had seen the Clay Street cable line being built and had kept himself informed on the developments. As Constructing Engineer, he managed the building of the line. In 1877 he decided to use concrete to construct the conduit and support the track. This was not only to strengthen the track, but also to circumvent the Hallidie patents. Later he applied for patents for this process, but had left it too long and was ruled out of time. He also made improvements to the track, winding house and grip, which he patented. He designed a new type of side grip, but the line crossed a number of existing cable lines requiring releasing and re-gripping the cable on twenty-two occasions and so the Eppelsheimer bottom grip proved more effective. The line itself opened in 1878.

In 1890 the system was extended and Root introduced a new design of tramcar. Previously there were two types of vehicle, the dummy car with the grip and some accommodation for passengers and the passenger trailer that carried most of the travellers. Henry Root designed a new type of tramcar combining the two functions. It was a passenger car that carried its own grip and driver. The car had an enclosed saloon in the centre with open sections at each end, all mounted on bogies. The basic principles of this design continue to be used today on the San Francisco cable lines.

ROSS, JAMES LEVESON 1848 – 1913

James Leveson Ross was born in Cromarty, Scotland, and he started a career in civil engineering after leaving Inverness Royal Academy, working on railways, harbour and water works. In 1868 he travelled to the United States of America to expand his career. He worked on a number of railways in America and Canada. In 1888, with his colleague and friend William Mackenzie, he worked on the conversion to electrical operation of the tramways of Montreal, Toronto and Winnipeg. In 1896 he and Mackenzie established the City of Birmingham Tramways Company in order to purchase the Birmingham Central Tramways Company. They converted the tramway from horse, accumulator and cable to electrical operation. He then looked to South America to expand his business interests. He became the first president of the Mexican Power Company that developed hydro-electric power.

SMITH, DAVID R. ? - ?

Hallidie engaged David Smith to undertake a survey of the route of a cable line up California Street in San Francisco. However, before it was entirely completed he had to leave in order to take up a job in South America. Hallidie took a break from his development of a cable tramway in San Francisco, picking it up later and deciding on a different route, that of Clay Street,

SMITH, JOB 1842 - ?

Job Smith, a native of Matlock, did not have an auspicious start in life. In 1852, at the age of 10, he started work as a bath attendant at Smedley's Hydro. The owner of the hydro, John Smedley, had a progressive attitude towards his staff, encouraging them to further their careers. Job Smith seems to have taken this to heart as he travelled to America to join the gold rush in California. It is said that he saw the Clay Street cable cars in San Francisco and he realised that this form of transport could be used on the steep hill of Matlock (however, there is incompatibility with dates, as he seems to have returned from America before the Clay Street line was built). When he returned to Matlock he set up the Malvern House Hydropathic Establishment in Smedley Street in 1890. It was his enthusiasm for the cable tram that persuaded Sir George Newnes to raise finance for the scheme and Smith was appointed as a Director of the tramway.

STANFORD, AMASA LELAND 1824 - 1893

Amasa Leland Stanford studied law and after graduating joined his brothers in the mercantile business. In 1861 he helped found the Central Pacific Railroad, becoming its president. He entered politics and became Governor of California in January 1862, returning to his railroad job in December 1863. In 1882 Stanford and his associates acquired the Market Street Railroad Company with the intention of converting it from horse haulage to cable operation and they renamed it the Market Street Cable Railway Company. It operated as a cable tramway until the death of Stanford in 1893. They changed the name back to the Market Street Railway Company and started conversion to electric power.

VON DONOP, PELHAM GEORGE (LIEUTENANT COLONEL) 1851 - 1921

Pelham George Von Donop was Chief Inspecting Officer of Railways for the Board of Trade and he was the Inspecting Officer for several of the British cable tramways.

WALKER, JAMES ? – 1910

James Walker was the engineer for the Isle of Man Harbour Commissioners. He undertook the formal inspection of the Upper Douglas Cable Tramway.

WHITE, GEORGE ? - ?

George White was the first manager of the Great Orme Tramway, a post he held for just two years. He had an argument with the directors over concerns he had about safety issues and the result was his dismissal. His concerns were realised some years later when the tramway had a fatal accident.

YERKES, CHARLES TYSON 1837 - 1905

Charles Yerkes had a chequered start to his working life, including a spell in prison for speculations with public money that went wrong. His sentence of 33 months was commuted to seven months after he revealed incriminating evidence on two prominent local politicians. On release he rebuilt his career and fortune continuing his profession as a broker for stock and grain. He moved to Chicago and became interested in public transport, particularly street railways. He was not averse to using less than scrupulous methods to achieve his aims. He purchased controlling interest in the North Chicago Street Railway followed by most of the other tramways in the City.

In 1886 he converted the North Chicago line from horse to cable operation followed by the other lines he controlled. His unscrupulous practices found no favour with the public. In 1900 he visited London and became involved in the development of the London underground system. He did not become involved in any British cable tramway.

YORKE, HORATIO ARTHUR, (LIEUTENANT COLONEL) 1848 - 1930

Lieutenant Colonel Arthur Yorke was an Inspector of Railways for the Board of Trade and he carried out the first inspection of the Swansea Constitution Hill tramway, failing it for public service until extensive remedial work was carried out. He rose to become the Chief Inspector of Railways in 1900.

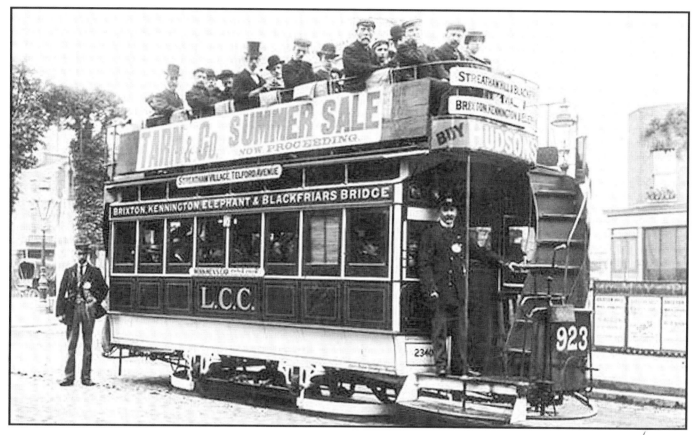

Above: A well patronised tramcar on the Brixton Hill route.

Below: A double deck tramcar passes the loop on the Highgate Hill tramway.

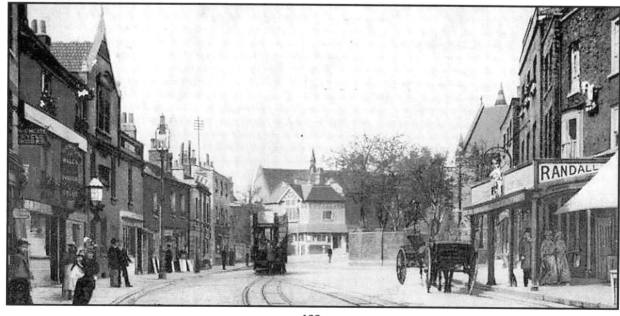

ACKNOWLEDGEMENTS

Once again, I am deeply obliged to Bob Appleton who, to my surprise, was not deterred when he proof read my "All Dressed Up and Somewhere to Go", and he agreed to proof read the final draft of this book. As always he has made valuable suggestions that have improved it, including the inspired title. However, all errors remain entirely my responsibility. Trevor Preece has applied his deft touch on my attempts at page design and impoved the book no end. Once again Adam Gordon has shown great fortitude in agreeing to publish yet another of my obscure missives.

In a rash moment, the Tramway and Light Railway Society agreed to my looking after the Society's digital photographic collection. I was amazed at how generous the members have been in allowing their photographic collections to be digitised and added to the collection; there are now in excess of 150,000 images. In addition to expanding the collection at every opportunity, I have been able to use the collection as a source of information and to choose some of the images to illustrate my books. To all these members I pass on my deep gratitude. In particular, my thanks go to Trevor Service for allowing me to use his photograph of the upper passing loop of the Great Orme tramway.

I would also like to thank all those tramway enthusiasts who have given me support, encouragement and information with this and all my other books. I am indebted to you all.

**This Edinburgh Northern Tramways Company crew proudly display their tramcar
from the 1890/92, 9—16 series.**